HISSES, BOOS, & CHEERS!

*(Or, A Pratical Guide To The Planning,
Producing and Performing of Melodrama!)*

by
Charles H. Randall and Joan LeGro Bushnell

With Illustrations by Howard Brewer

The Dramatic Publishing Company
311 Washington St., Woodstock, Illinois 60098

ISBN 0-87129-421-4

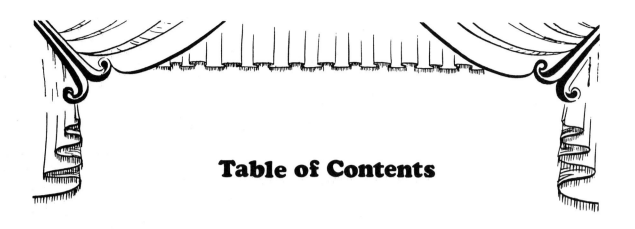

Table of Contents

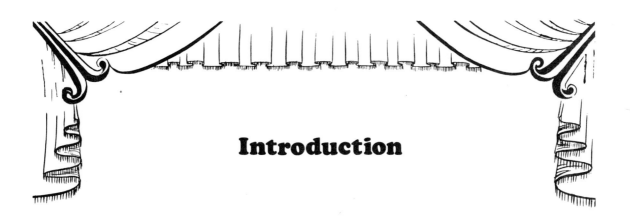

Introduction

WHY MELODRAMA?

Melodrama tends to suffer a rather shoddy reputation. Theatrical elitists often treat melodrama like an unwashed relative — one they feel reluctantly obliged to acknowledge at weddings and family reunions, but when the party is over they count the silver and sterilize the doorknobs! Such a reputation is absolutely not justified! The fact is that melodrama has been in the theatrical family from the very beginning, and has been a generous contributor to all of its relatives. It deserves appropriate recognition.

If we accept the common equation which states that *tragedy* is to *melodrama* as *high comedy* is to *farce*, we acknowledge that melodrama is a distinct entity and not just a failed attempt at tragedy. Melodrama implies a degree of exaggeration for the purpose of dramatic effectiveness. Farce implies a degree of exaggeration for the purpose of comic effectiveness. The old-fashioned melodrama that we are dealing with in this book is actually a delicate blend of both elements. When performed in that manner, melodramas have a spectacular track record of audience appeal.

The element of audience participation involved is a popular draw. Audiences find it entertaining to pitch in and cheer the hero and hiss the villain. It is that appeal which pulls audiences into the melodrama theatre, including an important segment for whom theatre-going is a new experience. We all know that without an audience there is no theatre. So, if your theatre group finds audiences dwindling and stubbornly reluctant to look beyond their television sets, a rousingly entertaining melodrama may very well "bring 'em back alive!"

The experience of performing melodramas for a large and lively audience is an excellent contribution to any actor's training. Like any other stylized departure from realism, melodrama requires a disciplined adjustment from the actor. He must learn to maintain flawless *concentration* under circumstances about as challenging as he is ever likely to encounter. He must learn that while working on a very broad scale, he must develop and maintain complete character *justification* for actions that are exaggerated and in situations that may border on the ludicrous. Working in melodramas helps the actor to develop that elusive but crucial element called *theatrical timing*. The demands on his voice and articulation are especially acute. He must adapt his *body movement* to a quality that serves the style.

In other words, melodrama is an exciting challenge to all of the actor's resources. The frosting on the cake is that it's fun to do — and not nearly as difficult as the foregoing catalogue of challenges might suggest. Perhaps because of the seeming lack of sophistication in the finished form, and aided by the element of audience participation, an inexperienced cast can, as a rule, achieve a higher level of success in a melodrama than in almost any other kind of theatre. And while they are doing it, they develop skills and disciplines that will serve them well in any other theatrical challenge.

Melodrama also has the advantage of offering experience opportunities for a broad but flexible segment of any group's casting pool. The need for extraneous or incidental olio entertainment as a part of the melodrama format allows a larger number of performers with a wide variety of skills to participate. Who knows? Perhaps this season's barbershop baritone may be next season's Hamlet!

WHAT IS MELODRAMA?

If we chide an over-zealous friend with, "Oh, don't be so melodramatic!" we are accusing him of emotional excess and of overstating his case. That reflects one of the many meanings or connotations which burden the word *melodrama*. Before we attempt an examination of one specific application of the word to denote a particular dramatic form, it might be helpful if we try to get *melodrama*, the word and the form, into some manageable perspective.

The traditional Western of film and television fame is almost pure melodrama with clearly drawn "good guys" and "bad guys" — the "white hats" and "black hats." We may be inclined to smile with amused condescension at the simple naivete of the cowboy film of two or three decades ago, but if we are really honest, we'll admit that most of these films still have the capacity to force us to hold our breath in tense anticipation as the "high noon" showdown nears, or to choke back a tear as the heroine's fate seems to be sealed.

Those cowboy films, as well as many modern films and television dramas, trade heavily on melodrama's clearly marked conflict between the forces of good and evil. They are also melodramatic in their reliance on heightened theatricality — startling and spectacular effects and often exaggeratedly high stakes in the struggle.

Melodramatic elements can be found in every period of theatrical history from Euripedes in ancient Athens to the movie you might see next week or next year. Shakespeare never heard the word melodrama (because it hadn't been coined yet), but his genius and showmanship made him understand the melodramatic effectiveness of Macbeth's encounter with the witches, or the appearance and disappearance of the ghost of Hamlet's father.

As a specific theatrical form, melodrama grew out of the eighteenth century, and became so immensely popular that it dominated the theatrical scene throughout the nineteenth century. The main impetus to its spectacular ascendancy came from the French pen of Rene Charles Guilbert de Pixerecourt (1773 – 1844) and his German counterpart, August Friederich Ferdinand von Kotzebue (1761 – 1819).

Kotzebue was a very prolific playwright who enjoyed a tremendous world-wide popularity at the start of the nineteenth century. He was highly skilled in the use of sentimentality, sensationalism, and spectacular theatrical effects.

It remained, however, for the slightly younger Frenchman, Pixerecourt, to intentionally shape these elements into a specific new theatrical form which became known as melodrama. The name comes from the French *melodrame*, a combination of words for song and drama. The plays of Pixerecourt — and of the host of imitators who followed — were literally plays with music. A special orchestration underscored the action in much the same way that a musical sound track accompanies and intensifies the action in a modern motion picture or television drama.

The form that emerged as nineteenth-century melodrama reflected a popular view that the sole purpose of drama was to "extol virtue and condemn vice." The popular plays of the period dealt almost exclusively with the struggle between the forces of good and evil. The struggle was always intense and perilous, and always resulted in the triumph of good over evil. The characters were one-dimensional types who were either good or bad. There were no grays on in-betweens. Comic relief was traditionally furnished by one or more comic characters who were inevitably associated with the forces of good. The villain was no laughing matter.

The most popular American melodrama of the nineteenth century was George L. Aiken's adaptation of Harriet Beecher Stowe's novel, *Uncle Tom's Cabin*, first produced in 1852. In this play, the institution of slavery, personified by Simon Legree, is the villain. On the side of the angels is pathetic Little Eva and Uncle Tom, simply but clearly drawn representatives of the forces of good. The resultant conflict became an enormously effective rallying cry for the cause of the abolitionists. So effective, in fact, in galvanizing public opinion that it has been said, with a degree of truth, that *Uncle Tom's Cabin* was instrumental in igniting the flames of the Civil War.

All nineteenth-century melodramas were, in a sense, dramatized lessons in morality or ethics. They frequently dealt with significant current issues. The post-Civil War era was a period in which alcohol abuse became a chronic domestic problem. The theatre responded with what became a vogue of very popular temperance plays. *The Drunkard* and *Ten Nights in a Barroom* were typical examples in which upstanding citizens are brought to the very brink of destruction by "Demon Rum," but regain health, wealth and self-respect when they take the pledge to abstain from strong drink. Both of these temperance dramas survive today in their original form and in contemporary adaptations, as popular fare for the modern audience. However, there is a vital difference! When properly presented, such tear-jerking dramas prove to be extremely amusing today.

Music used in conjunction with melodrama is most commonly thought of as belonging to the Gay Nineties, although any music dating to this period or prior to it is historically accurate.

The period of peace following the Civil War brought prosperous years during the late nineteenth century, and a fair share of this prosperity was directed toward the pursuit of entertainment. By the mid-1890's, about seventy-five million Americans owned one million pianos. The young lady or gentleman who could offer after-dinner selections on the parlour grand became the center of attention. Everyone gathered 'round, and sheet music sales boomed.

Many popular songs were composed by entertainers and carried across the miles by fellow showmen, thereby gaining exposure to a large audience. In many cases, it was only after a song had caught on with the general public that it would be published. Often, then, the song was ascribed to the performer who had popularized it rather than to its composer. As a result of this, the names of many songwriters from this period have been lost.

The music of the Gay Nineties may be divided into two very broad categories — classical and popular. Classical music was, as it is today, that which appealed to a more highly cultivated element of the population. The popular music of the time consisted of songs (music with words) which were written by and appealed to the general public. Because the term "Gay Nineties" describes an era which is not entirely confined to the decade from which it takes its name, most musical collections titled as such will be found to include songs from the turn of the century and the early nineteen hundreds.

The *melo* in melodrama applies not only, as many think, to musical numbers within the body of the play such as those heard in musical comedy; the term also refers to a continuing accompaniment woven throughout the dialogue of the play. This *incidental* music, as it is called, is intended to underscore and heighten the dramatic action, much as that heard in the sound tracks of modern-day movies and television.

Old-fashioned melodramas — both actual revivals and latter-day reconstructions — are genuine crowd pleasers. However, their successful production requires a careful balance between historical authenticity and subtle parody — performed with rigorous theatrical honesty. This book will examine principles and practices required to achieve such a balance. Throughout this book, the word *melodrama*, unless otherwise specified, refers to nineteenth -century melodrama — authentic or latter-day fabrications — which intentionally solicit audience participation in the form of cheers for the hero and hisses and boos for the antics of the villain.

Note:
The authors wish to
express their appreciation
to the following:
Greg Amerind, Howard Brewer,
Ron Harlan and Sue Dunbar White.

CHAPTER I

To The Director

As with any directorial undertaking, the melodrama director's job begins with a thorough study of the play at hand. In fact, if the current project happens to be the director's first melodrama production, it would be worth the time and effort to begin by reading a number of other typical melodramas to develop a comfortable familiarity with this particular kind of theatre.

Such a survey will make it clear that melodrama has more in common with other kinds of plays than it has unique differences. The typical structure of a melodrama is actually a *reductio ad absurdum* of the traditional "well-made play" composition. It is an oft-repeated maxim that "the essence of drama is conflict." That can quite accurately be paraphrased to read: "the essence of conflict is melodrama." The difference, where there is one, is not in substance, but in degree.

A playwright once responded to a "How do you write a play?" query with a rather caustic oversimplification: "In the first part, you get your hero up a tree. In the second part, you throw rocks at him, and in the last part, you either knock him out of the tree, or you let him climb down and flatten his attacker." That "nut-shell" observation can apply to everything from *Agamemnon* to *The Zoo Story*. In the case of melodramas, of course, the hero always gets out of the tree. That fact alone, however, does not make it a melodrama.

The principal difference between melodrama and other kinds of theatre is that other kinds seek to strike some balance between *what* is happening (the conflict) and to *whom* it is happening (character delineation). Melodrama is quite content to settle for easily recognized character types with little or no concern for subtle or unique psychological motivations. The hero and heroine are spotlessly pure; the villain is relentlessly evil. The melodrama focuses on the conflict between them — and inevitably leads the villain to ultimate defeat.

The first question, then, that the director asks at the beginning of the pre-rehearsal homework is, "What is the basic conflict?" That is actually the initial question in approaching any play, but in the case of a melodrama it is both more urgent and more easily answered. The opposing forces are, by definition, pure, simple and conspicuous.

Since subtitles such as theme, idea and point-of-view are rarely of significant concern in the case of an old-fashioned melodrama, those implied questions can be slighted or answered with a blanket statement to the effect that such melodramas exist primarily (in most cases, exclusively) to amuse or entertain an audience. The director's analysis, at this point, should focus on a precise determination of script elements that offer amusement or entertainment. The question here is, quite simply, "What's in it for the audience?" Arriving at an articulate answer to this involves the discovery of exactly how the basic conflict has been structured, when the elastic of suspense can be stretched most effectively, and where audible audience reactions can be reasonably anticipated.

A very useful sense of the structure of conflict can be achieved by a careful look at the playwright's craft. This is the time to remind ourselves that the second syllable of the word play*wright* means a construction worker, or one who builds something, as in millwright or shipwright. A playwright is both an artist and an artisan, a craftsman who builds plays. The basic construction unit or building block used by the playwright is called the *French scene*. This is quite different from the play segment normally itemized in the program as, for example, Act I, Scene 2 to indicate a change of time or place. The term French scene indicates only a change in the identity of characters on the stage. It takes its name from the seventeenth-century French practice of enumerating a new scene each time a principal character entered or left the stage. The neo-classic French playwrights (Corneille, Racine, et al) established this practice as a part of their effort to emulate their ancient Greek models. It is useful to us, however, for quite a different reason.

When a playwright brings a certain set of characters onto the stage to interact, it is to accomplish some specific dramatic purpose. That purpose, generally, constitutes one or more *events*. When that event has occurred, or the purpose accomplished, normally the playwright must arrange for one or more of the characters to leave the stage and/or different characters to enter. When this happens, a new French scene ensues. Each such character encounter constitutes an event in the series of events used by the playwright to introduce the conflict, develop it to its saturation point (the climax), and finally to resolve it.

Although there are undoubtedly as many techniques for writing plays as there are playwrights, one way or another the preliminary process must entail some planning. Formally or informally, explicitly or tacitly, the playwright must devise some kind of scenario or rough outline sequence of action or events with which the play will be built. When we break an existing play down to its French scene components and formulate an articulate statement of the basic action that takes place in each of the French scenes, we have reduced the play to a manageable scenario. This process can show us exactly how the playwright has put the play together. In effect, we disassemble the play.

The act of disassembling or "unwriting" a play can give us a surprising range of useful information. For example, study Figure 1 on page 14. This is a graphic projection of the French scene structure of Act One of the authors' melodrama, *Trapped by a Treacherous Twin or Double Trouble*!! (Dramatic Publishing Company, 1982)

The numbers on the horizontal axis at the top of the chart represent page numbers. The list of characters appearing in the act is perpendicular to the page numbers. When a character is onstage with lines, there are diagonal lines in the square representing that page opposite the character's name. An entrance or exit within a given page is indicated by the relative portion of the square at which the diagonal lines begin or end. This chart, for example, shows that the character named Yule makes his first entrance in the lower part of page 9 in the script. If a character is onstage without dialogue, the page square is marked with an X instead of diagonal lines. The chart shows that this is true of Toinette on page 10 and of Sadie on page 41. It is not uncommon to meet a situation in which a playwright has, sometimes accidentally, left a character onstage with no dialogue for an excessive period of time. This can pose a problem for both the director and the actor. A chart such as this one will pinpoint the problem and director and actor can be forewarned and forearmed.

Referring once more to the chart, we see that this particular play begins on page 5 with Grace onstage alone. Except for brief appearances by Toinette (we might well guess that she is the French maid), Grace remains alone until Sadie arrives near the bottom of page 7 and a new French scene begins.

By turning the page onto its vertical axis, we can read a simple statement of the action that takes place in each of the French scenes. These simplified statements, read in sequence, complete our process of "unwriting" the play because they read very much like the preliminary scenario or rough outline from which the finished play emerged.

With a bit of practice, it becomes a simple matter to produce such a chart

TRAPPED BY A TREACHEROUS TWIN
or
Double Trouble!!

Figure 1

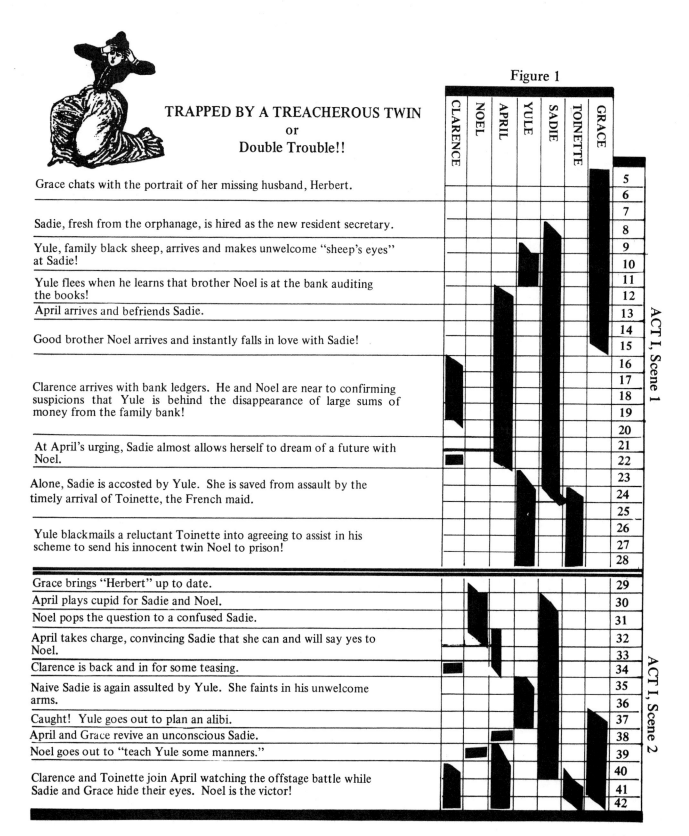

Grace chats with the portrait of her missing husband, Herbert.

Sadie, fresh from the orphanage, is hired as the new resident secretary.

Yule, family black sheep, arrives and makes unwelcome "sheep's eyes" at Sadie!

Yule flees when he learns that brother Noel is at the bank auditing the books!

April arrives and befriends Sadie.

Good brother Noel arrives and instantly falls in love with Sadie!

Clarence arrives with bank ledgers. He and Noel are near to confirming suspicions that Yule is behind the disappearance of large sums of money from the family bank!

At April's urging, Sadie almost allows herself to dream of a future with Noel.

Alone, Sadie is accosted by Yule. She is saved from assault by the timely arrival of Toinette, the French maid.

Yule blackmails a reluctant Toinette into agreeing to assist in his scheme to send his innocent twin Noel to prison!

Grace brings "Herbert" up to date.

April plays cupid for Sadie and Noel.

Noel pops the question to a confused Sadie.

April takes charge, convincing Sadie that she can and will say yes to Noel.

Clarence is back and in for some teasing.

Naive Sadie is again assulted by Yule. She faints in his unwelcome arms.

Caught! Yule goes out to plan an alibi.

April and Grace revive an unconscious Sadie.

Noel goes out to "teach Yule some manners."

Clarence and Toinette join April watching the offstage battle while Sadie and Grace hide their eyes. Noel is the victor!

ACT I, Scene 1

ACT I, Scene 2

14

for any play you may be preparing to direct. In its present form, the chart is a refinement of an earlier simple logistic tool designed to aid in the efficient scheduling of rehearsals for large-cast, complex musical productions. While that is still a useful "fringe benefit," the uses of the chart transcend mere logistics. Many directors find that the very act of laying out such charts contributes to a clear sense of the basic rhythm of a play — the ebb and flow of theatrical dynamics.

For example, the chart and resultant scenario shown in Figure 1 give us important clues about the play even without the full script in hand. We see immediately how the basic conflict involving Sadie and the twin brothers, Noel and Yule, is developed. Sadie is first repulsed by the unwelcome attentions of Yule, then captivated by the affections of Noel in alternate French scenes throughout Act I. In Act I, Scene 1, just when the heroine Sadie is about to believe happiness could be in store for her, the villain Yule makes an overt move that foretells disaster. Rhythmically, that pattern is repeated with ascending intensity in Act I, Scene 2. The act ends with an offstage confrontation between Noel and Yule.

Of course, that structural sequence is detectable by a reasonably practiced eye simply by reading the script. However, breaking the play down in this manner lays the parts out with graphic clarity. It becomes an almost automatic process to adjust the intensity of the villain's aggression from mildly annoying for Sadie in their first encounter (pages 9 and 10) to acutely alarming in their second meeting (pages 23 through 25), and to violently frightening in their third encounter in Scene 2 (pages 35 and 36). Pursuing the analytic process in this manner equips the director with an articulate sense of how to orchestrate the dramatic dynamics of the script for maximum effectiveness.

We must remember, of course, that the chart is not a complete portrait of the play. At most, it is an X-ray exposure which shows the bones that can allow the play to stand. It is the task of the director and the many collaborators to put the flesh and blood on those bones, and to breathe the appropriate sense of life into the production.

The process of "fleshing out" the bones can get an important assist from the act of phrasing the statement of action that accompanies the French scenes. While the sample chart limits its comments to scenario-like capsulization of the story-line action in each French scene, that is only a beginning of the potential for the process. It can — and should — be extended as far as the creativity of the director allows. It is an excellent discipline to develop the habit of keeping a director's notebook. Once you have phrased the caption or action statement for a given French scene, think about it and toy with it until you are certain that it captures the essence of action that you see in the scene. Enter the statement on your play chart and also at the top of a nice blank page in your notebook. Every time you reread the play (that should be many, many times in this pre-rehearsal stage) keep the notebook handy to jot down ideas, impressions, images and actions under the appropriate French scene captions. You may find yourself jotting down ideas that strike you as silly ten minutes later. That is perfectly all right! Draw a line through them if you feel like it. It's probably not a good idea, however, to completely obliterate the rejected idea — it may contain a useful germ of an idea that will resurface later. In any case, treat your notebook like a fluid, shifting journal of thought — designed essentially for your eyes only. You will soon discover that every idea you have put into your notebook — great or small, profound or petty, noble or inane — will ultimately contribute to the ease and effectiveness of every subsequent phase of your directorial work on the production. You will go into rehearsal fully attuned to the overall thrust of the play and comfortably knowledgeable about the size, shape and texture of every one of the building blocks from which the play is made.

A. Gearing Up

Your pre-rehearsal preparations can be very exciting — but sometimes very lonely. As that phase gives way to the collective activities such as production meetings, tryouts and rehearsals, that feeling of loneliness may begin to look pretty good in retrospect! Theatre is always a collaborative enterprise: that is one of its features that makes theatre so compellingly attractive for most of us. But unless you are superhuman, you may find yourself, at times, harboring a secret wish that "they would all go away!" If you *do* reach that point, you had better keep the wish to yourself and pray that no one reads your mind! You need them all!

The collaboration will be smoother and inevitably more successful if each participant has a clear perspective of the nature and dimension of the production project. At the outset, it should be spelled out as concretely as possible exactly what contribution is expected from each and exactly *when* each production phase *must* be completed. In other words, a production organization must be *organized*!

The actual scope of such an organization varies wildly, ranging from the typical university theatre where every production area is headed by a faculty member who is a highly trained professional to the small high school where the responsibilities of the teacher/director can be summed up in a single word: *everything*!

Regardless of where, within that range, your particular organization falls, the responsibility for the ultimate success of the production rests with you, the director. It is normally up to you to see that the wheels of progress start on time, are all turning in the same direction and that the whole contraption is aimed at the same target!

A.1) Organization

If a production organization isn't already in place as an ongoing part of your group's structure, you will have to start very early to scrounge, coerce and cajole until a production staff can be put together. Whether you are blessed with a wealth of talented and eager co-creators or faced with a personnel pool that barely rates as a puddle, there are certain jobs that must be done — certain functions that must be fulfilled before the play can open. Figure 2, the organizational chart on page 18, illustrates a typical organization necessary for the production of a melodrama. If each indicated position can be filled with a qualified collaborator, you are off to a flying start. It is much more probable, however, that you and some of your colleagues will have to "double in brass" by filling more than one position. It is usually unfortunate, however, when the director, by choice or by force, attempts to wear too many hats. Unless you are an authentic Renaissance person with unlimited talent, resources and energy, it is important that you delegate as much of the support staff responsibility as possible. Spreading yourself too thin will inevitably result in shortchanging the production, the cast and — worst of all — the audience.

A.2) Production Meetings

Once you have your production organization established, one of the most important parts of your work begins. You are captain of the ship and the

Figure 2

A TYPICAL ORGANIZATIONAL CHART

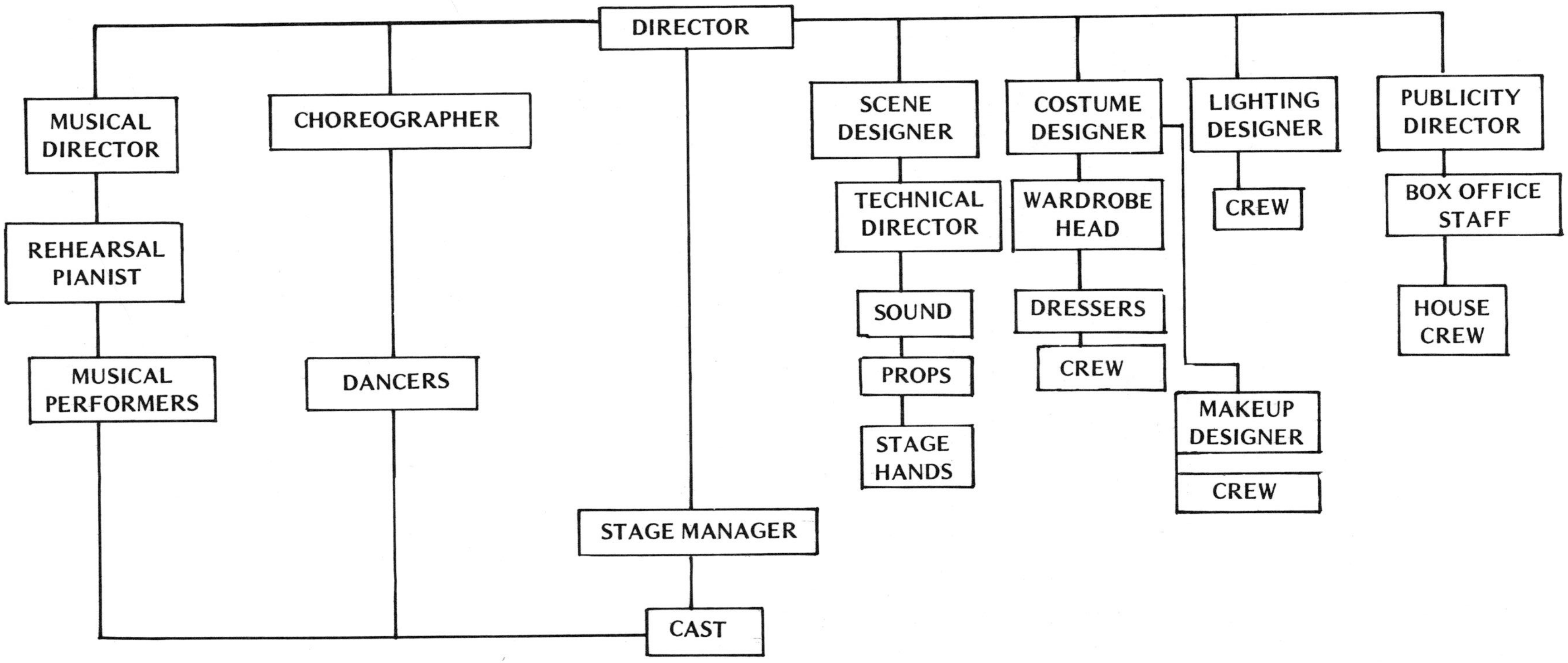

```
                                    DIRECTOR
        ┌───────────────┬───────────────┼───────────────┬───────────────┬───────────────┐
   MUSICAL        CHOREOGRAPHER      SCENE          COSTUME          LIGHTING        PUBLICITY
   DIRECTOR                          DESIGNER       DESIGNER         DESIGNER        DIRECTOR
      │               │                │               │               │               │
  REHEARSAL        DANCERS        TECHNICAL        WARDROBE          CREW          BOX OFFICE
  PIANIST                         DIRECTOR         HEAD                             STAFF
      │                               │               │                               │
  MUSICAL                          SOUND           DRESSERS      MAKEUP           HOUSE
  PERFORMERS                                                     DESIGNER         CREW
                                   PROPS            CREW           CREW

                                   STAGE
                                   HANDS

                 STAGE MANAGER

                     CAST
```

success of the voyage will be greatly influenced by the articulate success with which you are able to share your ideas, conceptions and objectives with your co-workers.

This is where your lonely pre-rehearsal preparations begin to pay off. Still well before tryout time, you will call the first of what will be a series of production meetings. This should be attended by all of the designers, the choreographer, the musical director and the publicity director. Each of these should have been previously equipped with a copy of the play. Each should attend this first production meeting armed with a fairly intimate familiarity with the script.

A.2a.) The Scene Designer

The very first item on the agenda for this meeting should be a discussion, under your leadership, of the *style* of production best suited to this particular melodrama. This will be a good time for you to assert your courage and leadership by disarming that word *style* before it can ricochet around the room inflicting semantic mayhem on the entire project. Defining *style* is an age-old enterprise that ranks right up with squaring the circle and inventing perpetual motion! Sir John Gielgud probably did it best when he said, "Style is knowing what kind of play you are in." That definition has the great virtue of disclaiming the entire cargo of mysticism and mumbo-jumbo that usually lurks in and around the word. We suggest that you stay pretty close to Sir John's beautiful simplicity. Let it be known that style will denote nothing more nor less than *the size and collective characteristics of the theatrical world the production will put on the stage, and the manner in which the people of that world relate to each other and to the people in the audience.*

The world of the old-fashioned melodrama is a careful blending of dramatic reality and blatant theatricality. The *reality* portion of that blend is a crucial ingredient. Without it, the whole enterprise disintegrates into some kind of inept silliness that is neither engaging nor amusing. We will discuss this vital element in greater detail later when we consider the work of the actor. For the moment, let us merely suggest that melodrama's world is not a re-creation or representation of actual nineteenth-century life, as such. Rather, it is a slightly exaggerated representation of life as it may have been on a *nineteenth-century* stage, presented to a twentieth-century audience.

It is that concept of *stage* reality that allows you and your scene designer to discuss the play's physical environment within a range of complexity to simplicity. You can select a style (or, if you prefer, *scenic treatment*) that is consistent with both the esthetic demands of the form and the limitations of technical resources available to you. Historically, the typical scenery for a nineteenth-century melodrama consisted of wings, borders and drops. The scenes painted on those drops were rendered with great skill and artistry — but they were *not* reality. Strictly speaking, they didn't even *look* like reality. It was theatrically sufficient that, for that audience, they *suggested* reality.

So, in this initial production meeting, you and your co-workers will be seeking to determine the kind of physical appearance your production will have. The important thing is that all parties concerned remember the difference between attempting to duplicate *real life* on the stage and *suggesting* (possibly with the artist's tongue slightly in his cheek) *stage life* of a real theatre of a bygone era. For instance, in a production of *Ten Nights in a Barroom*, the scene in Joe Morgan's home where his little daughter Mary is about to surrender her spirit to the angels could be depicted as an almost infinite variety of ways. Mary's bed is the dominant element in this scene. The rear wall could be a drop on which is painted the cracks in the plaster, the headboard of the bed, and a framed embroidered motto hanging slightly askew. Or if you have decided, for reasons of fiscal or esthetic economy, to play the entire show in front of neutral drapes with minimal set pieces, the bed may carry its own headboard and the framed embroidered motto may hang from overhead wires. In either case, you would be making a visual statement which recognizes the distinction between realism and theatrical truth.

Once a style has been determined, there remain a number of practical decisions which can be arrived at rather easily. You will have to let your designer know exactly what ground plan requirements you see for each act or scene, i.e. the number and location of entrances and exits, etc. Having worked with the structural analysis chart (Figure 1), you will be able to pinpoint any particular physical requirements for action or business which the set would have to accommodate. For example, in *Trapped by a Treacherous Twin*, Act I, Scene 2, the hero Noel has a fistfight with the villain Yule. Since these two are twin brothers played by the same actor, that fight has to take place offstage. The action requires French doors in the back wall of the set, through which other characters observe the fight and furnish a blow-by-blow description. Clearly that special requirement effectively eliminates the option of a painted drop for that play. The French doors could, of course, be designed as a part of a series of framed flats as a traditional scenic rear wall of a box set or they could be incorporated into neutral drapes very easily. But one way or another, those French doors are required for that play and they had better be discussed at that first production meeting.

A.2b.) The Costume Designer

There are, of course, a host of other decisions to be made at this first production meeting. Costume requirements need to be discussed at this time. The organization of the group and the specific requirements of the play may have already answered the first costume question: Where are the costumes coming from? Are they to be designed and created? Purchased? Rented? Borrowed or scrounged from Aunt Hattie's attic? Or, perhaps, a little of all of those options. If your group is such that there is no one designated as costume designer, *per se*, you had better move heaven and earth to see to it that the very best qualified person available is designated as *costume coordinator*. It is a sad commentary on some amateur theatres that costume considerations are all too often ignored or given such a low priority that grotesquely unfortunate decisions are made at the very last minute. Such neglect, be it ever so benign, is bound to have an effect on the production that ranges from embarrassing to disastrous. And the odds strongly favor disastrous!

Costumes are a conspicuous visual element in theatre which is a conspicuous visual art. (We go to *hear* a concert, but we go to *see* a play!) When you and I meet people in our daily lives, we make quick and often subconscious judgments about them based on the clothes they wear. Audiences do the same with characters they see on the stage. Such judgments are not limited to the surface statistical factors like age, social status, profession, etc. Audience members also feed their subliminal mental computers reams of costume-based data of such diverse nature as personality traits of the character, chronological setting of the play, and esthetic implications such as the degree of seriousness or frivolity invited by the character and the play.

When we spoke of scenery for melodramas, we made the point that the goal was a *suggestion* of reality as it may have appeared on the *stage* in an earlier time. The same observation can be made in the case of melodrama costumes. Absolute historical accuracy is seldom if ever the objective for any kind of theatre costumes. It should most certainly *not* be the target for melodrama costumes! As with scenery, we are seeking a sense of heightened theatricality.

Color, line, texture and trim are important tools that the costumer uses to achieve that theatrical flair. Of course, if your costumes are being begged, borrowed or scrounged, there may be a very limited degree of control over these factors — but care can and must still be used in coordinating the costumes.

Just because Mary Sue looks absolutely adorable in that bright red dress she found in grandmother's trunk does not mean that it would be a good costume for her — especially if she happens to be playing the heroine!

Those responsible for the planning and execution of costumes, scenery, properties and lighting should use these production meetings as forums in which all aspects of the technical production are articulated and coordinated. Costumes must be planned in close cooperation with the planning of the scenery. Costumes that are too close to the color of the sets tend to make the actors disappear. Both the costumer and the set designer had better be aware of the obligation to coordinate their color palettes. That "perfect" Victorian sofa could turn out to be a visual disaster if its green upholstery fights the colors of the sets or costumes.

Not only must the costume colors harmonize with the total visual composition, they serve to delineate and heighten character qualities. Since melodrama deals with rather broadly drawn characters who are, for the most part, clearly identified as being either good or evil, costume statements must be broad and clear. The villain needs to *look* like the villain! His costume, like his heart, is traditionally black. Beware of deciding to play the show in front of black drapes. You may find yourself with a villain that seems to be a strange disembodied face floating in space! It is fun to stick with the melodramatic tradition of dressing your villain in a black cape which can be lined with a bright red material.

The hero, strong-hearted, bold and true, should be dressed to project those qualities. Putting the hero in a dark suit that is visually too near to the villain's can create almost insurmountable problems for the actor — and the audience. The heroine's costume must make it instantly clear that she is as "pure as the driven snow!" However, a pure white dress will pose real problems for the lighting designer. White under stage lights has a tendency to "bounce" so much that it can become hard for the audience to watch. It is frequently preferable to put the heroine in light colors, but not actually white. If you start with a washable white fabric, it can be given a light dye rinse or be dipped in a tea solution which will pull it subtly toward an off-white, and generally take care of the problem of glare from bouncing light.

Costumes must also function to keep the dominant characters visually dominant within a scene. Care must be taken to avoid a situation in which a subordinate character is put onstage in a costume which "steals the scene." It is not uncommon to see an amateur production in which the principals have clearly been costumed with care and taste, but which includes a crowd scene which seems to have been costumed in whatever was left over. That beautiful yellow dress may be a joy to behold, but if it tends to call undue attention to itself, to pull the wearer out of the crowd, it becomes a negative value and ought to be changed.

Above all else, the costumes must serve the actor. It must become a part of the character the actor is creating. A costume that is inappropriate because it fails to project or reinforce the character robs the actor, robs the production, and robs the audience. A costume that is ill-fitting or so constructed as to inhibit the actor's freedom of movement can make it impossible for that actor to be effective onstage. The actor's work demands his or her total concentration. The villain should not be forced to divide his concentration between abducting the heroine and keeping his shirt studs from popping open or his cape from falling off! The performer also deserves a break in regard to the mechanics of costumes. If the play calls for an offstage change of costume, it should be as efficient and effortless as possible. All too often, the time allowed for the change is absolutely minimal. No performer should be asked to cope with hooks and eyes or tiny buttons while negotiating a ninety-second costume change! Such fastenings may be fine for street dress, but they should be avoided in costumes. Niceties such as Velcro fastenings can usually accommodate or facilitate quick changes, save the show, the performer's equilibrium and the director's sanity!

A.2c.) The Lighting Designer

One of the important functions of this first production meeting is to bring the principal collaborators together for a declaration of *inter*dependence. The costumer and scenic artist, as we have seen, must work closely together and their combined work should be enhanced by appropriate color and quality of light. The person responsible for designing the lights for your melodrama production should be a very active participant in this early exchange of ideas about form and color. The final decisions about lights — especially the selection of color media — will happen somewhat later in the production process, but they will be made largely on the basis of related choices which start to take shape here.

Because melodrama suggests a rather simplified view of life as it might have been seen on the *stage* in an age less complex than our own, its lighting demands tend to be rather simple and straightforward. Typically, today's melodrama deals with the last decade or so of the nineteenth century. That was a time when electric lighting was only beginning to make its theatrical debut. While its potential was generating excitement among world theatre leaders, its full utilization as a creative tool was still a few years away. Most of us think of the Gay Nineties as a gas-lit era. Theatrically speaking, that connotation is essentially accurate. The visual flavor of that theatre can be suggested without elaborate or sophisticated lighting facilities.

Assuming that your production will be presented on a proscenium stage as opposed to an arena or "in-the-round," an easy suggestion of the early gas light era can be made by the addition of footlight sconces or shields. These are simply curved pieces of metal cut in a semi-circular or shield shape and mounted vertically along the footlights or at the edge of the apron. They should be spaced at intervals of twelve to eighteen inches and should be from eight to twelve inches high. The height of these footlight shields should be checked carefully to make sure that they pose no significant sight-line problems for front row patrons.

Footlights, or at least the appearance of footlights, carry an almost nostalgic suggestion of a bygone era. But even with the sham footlight shields along the front of the stage, your lighting designer may be reluctant to incorporate actual footlights into the design. Modern lighting practice rarely includes them because they tend to distort actors' faces into grotesque gargoyles. If they are to be used in your production, be sure that there is ample facility for front lighting to counter the awkward shadows and unnatural highlights that footlights can create. It would normally require at least six ellipsoidal reflector instruments to achieve minimal front lighting. If this is available, then full use of footlights behind those stylized shields can effectively contribute to the illusion of old-time theatricality. An alternative is to conceal a few miniature or baby spots behind the shields and make selective use of them for special accent lights.

As a rule, lighting for melodrama should avoid extreme or self-conscious effects likely to call undue attention to themselves. However, lighting can score melodramatic points for the audience. For instance, when the hero and heroine are smitten by Cupid's darts and pause for that long moment while the incidental music gives audible testimony to their romantic "condition," lighting can add to the impact. Exactly at the time the incidental music begins, hit the couple with a special warm pink light. If done with some subtlety, the remaining area lights can be dimmed slightly and the romantic interlude can become a show stopper!

The most important thing to remember about lighting in general — and melodrama lighting specifically — is that its primary function is to provide visibility. It can and does, of course, contribute to the compositional unity of the stage and enhance mood, but visibility must not be sacrificed to either of these ends.

Normally, melodrama is not the place to experiment with highly contrasting lighting or the use of spectacular intense colors. Barring extraordinary circumstances, a very limited supply of colored gels will get the job done. Your inventory should include a few shades each of a warm and a cool color. All should be very light colors. The warms can be a range of pinks or from straw to a light amber. The cools should be in a range from light blue to sky blue.

It is standard practice to divide the stage into six major areas for lighting purposes. Each of these areas is then lit from two sides at approximately a forty-five degree angle. One of the two lights for each area is a cool color and the other is warm.

Incidentally, it is good practice to mount two small spotlights in the area where the actors apply their makeup. These should be gelled with the colors used onstage. This allows the cast to check makeup and costume under stage lighting.

The foregoing technical considerations are typical of the agenda items which should be aired at the first production meeting. That meeting is an occasion for a mutual exploration of approaches and a unified style of production. The meeting is a point of departure for the melodrama. Details and specifics will evolve as each participant works out the implementation of his or her con-

Figure 3

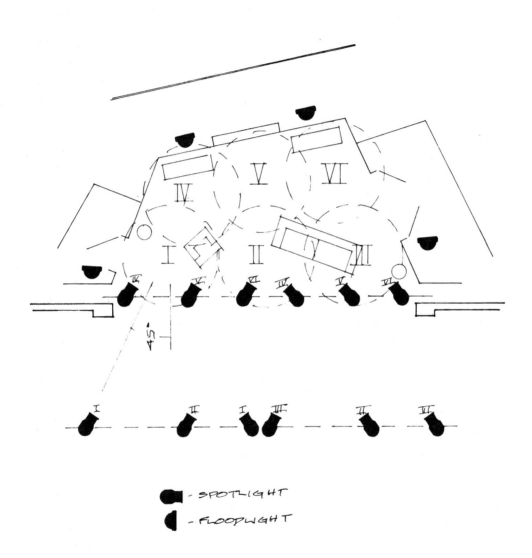

tribution. Those details and specifics should be shared as appropriate in subsequent production meetings. You, and all of your key collaborators, should be kept abreast of developments as they occur. To this end, production meetings should be scheduled on a regular basis – probably once a week until the melodrama opens. A word of caution, however. No prudent director will call a meeting just for the sake of a meeting if there is neither an agenda nor a purpose! Since Aeschylus first walked off with the laurels in Athens, there has never been a theatre production that couldn't have used a "bit more time!" Time is always at a premium. Do not waste it!

B. Tryouts

All of your early homework and preliminary production meeting with your behind-the-scenes collaborators have been preparing for the next crucial step: selecting the performers who will add flesh and blood to the playwright's work and significance to the whole enterprise. Many directors, like most actors, approach tryouts with emotions somewhere between dread and sheer terror. Because this step in the process is so very important, you should do everything in your power to conquer or conceal any personal fears or misgivings you may have at this time. One very productive technique for transcending your personal discomfort is to concentrate your efforts on contributing to the comfort of everyone else involved.

Acting always involves an element of exposure and vulnerability. Tryouts tend to create a maximum vulnerability. Even seasoned professionals can trigger an ulcer attack just thinking about the process. Beginners can be paralyzed into ineffectuality or driven away before you have a chance to see their potential. In either case, everyone loses. It is important that you do everything in your power to see that those who come to tryouts find an atmosphere that is friendly, warm and efficient.

It is a good idea to enlist one or two of your most reliable regulars to serve as informal greeters at the tryouts. Such greeters should be particularly alert to make newcomers feel welcome. Nothing is more destructive to the ongoing health of any producing group than a reputation – real or imagined – for being an exclusive or "hard-to-crack" club.

Preparations for the tryouts should include a well-planned program of advanced publicity. It is extremely important that every potential candidate has timely notification, not only of *where* and *when*, but also a pretty clear idea of *what*. Handbills, bulletin board displays, assembly skits and interviews in school and/or local newspapers are a few of the possible avenues for getting the word out. Regulars in your group should be encouraged to take an active part in publicizing the tryouts. They can do more than anyone else to let it be known that being in a play can be exciting, rewarding and a whole lot of fun. If you are working within the format of a drama club, it can be profitable to offer a reward or recognition for the regular member who brings the greatest number of newcomers to tryouts.

When a candidate walks into tryouts, there is an immediate need for an exchange of information. At that moment, the candidate is wary and plagued with uncertainties. Any concrete information about the play or the tryout process tends to be a settling influence. At the same time, you will need to have some information about each candidate at your fingertips.

Your student greeters should have dittoed handouts for everyone. The handout should contain a brief synopsis of the play, a full description of each character in the play and a projected schedule of rehearsals and performances. This handout will, in most cases, be the candidate's first tangible contact with the production. It should be carefully prepared with a bit of salesmanship included in its preparation. The play synopsis should be done with a bit of flair that suggests the flavor of sheer fun that can be involved in the performance of a melodrama. Likewise, the character descriptions should be presented in such a way that the potential of smaller roles is stressed. The "star" mentality, the "lead role or nothing" syndrome, is counterproductive and should be actively discouraged in any amateur production.

The structure of a typical melodrama actually helps to defuse that dangerous "lead or nothing" approach. Unlike some straight dramas, melodramas usually offer four or five "meaty" roles that are approximately equal in size. There are, by definition, the hero, the heroine, the villain, and usually a principal comic and/or a villain's accomplice who reforms in the course of the play. With the normal balance among those roles, it is less likely that a single "lead" looms as the only casting plum. It is also usually possible to offer olio participation as a means of minimizing the differences between the "big parts" and "small parts."

At the same time that such pertinent data is being distributed, each candidate should receive an information blank to fill out for you. Of course the exact nature of the needed information may differ from one organization or situation to another. A typical example of a tryout information sheet is shown in Figure 4, page 30.

Some directors prefer to delay making scripts available until after tryouts so that everyone is on an equal footing with a cold reading. Others make a point of having the scripts available well in advance and well publicized so that candidates can be expected to arrive at the tryouts with some degree of familiarity with the play. While there is merit in both positions, we strongly favor doing everything possible to get all interested parties to read the play before tryouts. In educational theatre, one frequently finds potentially strong actors who are simply miserable at cold readings. If such a student is denied the opportunity to read the play in advance, his or her potential may well be overlooked and a real asset lost to the production.

Of course, just having the scripts available for a period of time before tryouts is not going to guarantee that your tryouts are going to be attended exclusively by talented and well-prepared actors! That condition may prevail somewhere in "that great theatre in the sky," but during our mortal tenure, we had better be prepared to cope with something less than the ideal! If an actor's quality catches your interest in spite of problems with reading, don't hesitate in asking him or her to put the script aside for a moment and to improvise with another actor in a situation which roughly parallels the script. You should be prepared to suggest the improvisational setup. Such activity should not necessarily be limited to the troubled readers. A brief assigned improvisation can frequently tell you a great deal about the actor's imagination and sense of stage presence.

In melodrama, the characters tend to be clearly drawn types with little or no subtle gray shadings. Because of this, your job of casting may appear to be a bit easier than in other kinds of drama. The handsome, fair-haired youth may walk onto the stage to read with "hero" written all over him. But do not jump too fast and do not succumb to tunnel vision that excludes other possibilities from your view. That handsome "hero" may or may not have the personal quality to interest an audience for two or more hours. He also may turn out to be half a head shorter than the actress who finally emerges as your obvious heroine! You must remain receptive, observant and open throughout the entire process.

As a part of your preparation for tryouts, you will have identified scenes or

Figure 4

〰〰〰〰〰〰〰
TRYOUT SHEET
〰〰〰〰〰〰〰

A NOTE FROM THE DIRECTOR:

Welcome! May I express my gratitude and that of Fine Arts Board of Directors. We value your participation. Of course, no theatre can exist without lots of energy and team-work. This is especially true of a venture such as ours. If you know of other members who may be waiting for an extra nudge to join us, won't you try a touch of friendly arm-twist-ing? We — and they — will be glad you did! — JLB

〰〰〰〰〰〰〰〰〰〰〰〰〰〰〰〰〰〰〰〰〰〰〰〰

NAME _____ PHONE _____

⎯⎯⎯⎯⎯⎯⎯⎯⎯⎯
(please print)

ADDRESS _____ HEIGHT _____ SHOE SIZE _____
⎯⎯⎯⎯⎯⎯⎯⎯
DRESS SIZE (WOMEN) _____

SUIT SIZE (MEN) _____

〰〰〰〰〰〰〰〰〰〰〰〰〰〰〰〰〰〰〰〰〰〰〰〰

(Please do not write in this space.)

〰〰〰〰〰〰〰〰〰〰〰〰〰〰〰〰〰〰〰〰〰〰〰〰
I WOULD LIKE TO BE CONSIDERED FOR THE THE FOLLOWING ROLES:

1) _____ 2) _____ 3) _____ 4) _____

I WOULD BE WILLING (and able?) TO SING AS A CHARACTER IN THE PLAY: Yes
No

I WOULD BE WILLING (and able?) TO DANCE AS A CHARACTER IN THE PLAY:
Yes   No

I WOULD BE WILLING TO TAKE PART IN AN OLIO NUMBER: Yes   No

Previous theatrical experience (NONE REQUIRED! If you don't have any, this will be a fun place to get some!):

〰〰〰〰〰〰〰〰〰〰〰〰〰〰〰〰〰〰〰〰〰〰〰〰
I WOULD BE GLAD TO PITCH IN AND HELP IN THE FOLLOWING AREA(S): Props
Set Construction   Stage Crew   Costumes   Makeup   Lights
Sound   Any place I'm needed.

Please indicate any commitments which would conflict with rehearsals on weekday evenings or Sunday afternoons.

excerpts which will let you hear and see each character in a variety of combinations with other characters. The analysis chart which you have prepared (See Figure 1, page 14.) will make it an easy matter to identify those excerpts. It is a good idea to use a maximum variety of scenes for tryout purposes. For instance, as you listen to various combinations of candidates for hero and heroine, use as many different hero/heroine excerpts as the scripts offer. Pair after pair reading the same scene has some built-in hazards. If one reader happens to get a particular response from the others present, you may find that subsequent readers, reading the same scene, will consciously or unconsciously, try to imitate what they have heard. That may give you a half-dozen versions of "Reader A" and not much of an idea of what the imitators can really do. Another problem is that repeated readings of the same scene are almost certain to get boring for everyone — yourself included! If you are human, hearing a variety of scenes will tend to increase your capacity for attentive and creative listening which is so vital to your function at tryouts!

Because of the demands for intense concentration for everyone involved, it is usually preferable to break the tryout process up into two or three shorter sessions rather than one marathon which leaves you and everyone else wrung-out and numb! If you have scheduled multiple tryout sessions, be sure that everyone understands. It can be a terrible blow to actor morale to sit through hours of tryouts waiting one's turn only to be told to "come back tomorrow." This is one of the immediate uses for those information sheets each actor filled out on arrival. Each time you hear a candidate read, pull his or her sheet from the original stack, make any appropriate notes and put the sheet in a different stack. The size of the original stack automatically tells you how many people you have not yet heard.

Even after you have heard everyone at least once, and have called for various combinations of readers for your own purposes, it is a good practice to reserve the final portion of any session to allow and encourage any candidate to read or reread for any character he or she may choose. This open session does tend to give everybody a fair chance. Do not allow yourself to get lethargic and tune this process out as though it were merely a prefunctory "bread and butter" obligation. You can often get some very pleasant surprises from actors you had overlooked or misjudged in earlier readings.

As the readings progress, you will very likely find that candidates are tending to fall into several distinct categories ranging from "very probable" through "could be" to "impossible." It is only natural that you will be asking those from the first two categories back for repeated readings in various combinations. Don't be surprised when you discover that some of the "very probable's" lose some luster in repeated readings, becoming less and less interesting and sliding quietly into "could be's" or even "impossible's."

This is the stage of tryouts when everyone present "knows" more about what you are thinking than you do! It may be unavoidable, but you would be well advised to keep a corner of your mind on the kind of "signals" those in attendance may *think* they are getting. You may have asked Mary Sue to read the heroine's part three times with different possible heroes, only to discover that she just does not project the quality of innocent naiveté that the role demands. However, the mere fact that she read three times may well kindle a mass assumption that Mary Sue has the part sewed up. Such "second-guessing" the director can have a very unfortunate effect on the reading performance of other candidates in whom you are actually very interested.

It is a better practice to save the more intense rereadings until a later session that has been specifically designated as a time for call-backs. The call-back policy has a number of distinct advantages. Not only does it help minimize the degree to which you unwillingly feed the rumor mills and second-guessers, but it gives you and everyone else a chance to sleep on it.

Particularly in educational theatre, casting decisions, once announced, are almost impossible to retract. Dropping a cast member during rehearsals simply because your judgment was faulty at tryout time can be devastating to the student as well as destructive to the morale of the rest of the cast. You really need a respite of detachment and quiet before making your selection. Use it to arrange your most promising casting possibilities into groups or combinations. With the black and white quality of characters in a melodrama, the element of contrast and compatibility is even more important than in other kinds of drama. The villain, for instance, will seem more menacing if he happens to be the tallest member of the ensemble. While it may not be possible for you to cast a villain with that kind of conspicuous physical advantage, you can keep the principle in mind as you contemplate various possible casting combinations. The heroine must have both the physical and aesthetic quality of innocent vulnerability. There must, of course, be a quality compatibility between the hero and heroine. It doesn't hurt a bit if they both happen to be light complexioned blonds. If the hero seems to project such a sense of power that he could flatten the villain with one hand, it will be more difficult for him to generate the kind of suspense and excitement that is inherent in every melodrama script.

With such tangible and intangible factors in mind, you should be able to zero in on a manageable list of finalists. Of course, if you find yourself in a situation in which you have six people trying for a play with eight roles, you have a totally different kind of problem. In that case, you'll just have to haunt the hallways or get on the telephone and drum up some more actors. Usually, however, you will have to go through some kind of process of elimination to arrive at a list of names to be posted for call-backs.

At the call-back readings, double check your judgment by pairing readers in various combinations until one ensemble begins to emerge as the most effective. It is good practice, before making any commitments or announcing any decisions, to get the entire ensemble onstage at one time. Check now for visual interest and appropriate reinforcement of the dynamics of the script. Will it be easy for this group to create clear projections of good guy/bad guy forces that are the essential ingredients in the melodrama? It is not necessary to rely on what is commonly called "type casting" for a melodrama. Your actors must be unique, well-rounded individuals. The characters are *types*. Your job here is to assemble a cast of interesting human beings who can create those theatrical types in a theatrically interesting manner.

C. Planning Your Rehearsal Schedule

There is no minimum or magic number of rehearsals required for the preparation of a melodrama. In fact, the rehearsal process is substantially the same as it is for any full-length production. Depending on the availability of cast and rehearsal space, and the limits on the length of individual rehearsals, somewhere in the vicinity of thirty rehearsals of about two and a half to three hours each is probably close to optimum. That is based on five rehearsals a week for six weeks. Extending the process over a greater stretch of calendar time carries the risk of exceeding the cast's energy span to the point that rehearsals become listless and counterproductive. Telescoping the process into much less calendar time, unless your cast is unusually talented and well trained, risks presenting an underprepared production with the cast functioning on raw nervous energy that borders on hysteria. Determination of your particular schedule will depend on your knowledge of your cast and your play. The trick is to lead your cast through a scheduled series of rehearsals in such a way that they are uniformly tuned and keyed to performance pitch precisely on opening night — certainly not later and, hopefully, not sooner!

The process of getting from the first rehearsal to the opening night is a journey that is always fascinating, although often exhausting, nerve-wracking and seemingly perilous. The actors look to you to pilot them through the "rocks and shoals" of the journey safely. That means that you must plan the trip carefully. To abandon our analogy of travel, another helpful way to think of the process is to compare it with the irising of a spotlight. At the first rehearsal, we begin with the iris wide open to take in the whole play. As rehearsals progress, we iris the spotlight in on smaller and smaller details. As we near the final stages of the rehearsal process, we again open the iris wider and wider until by opening night we are once more dealing not with minutia but with the whole.

Every director learns to allocate rehearsal time in a way that reflects individual or personal tastes and methodology. But regardless of individual differences, rehearsal periods tend to fall into four basic divisions. First, a period of blocking in which you deal with the meaning (intelligence) and movement inherent in the script. Secondly, a period, usually the longest of the four divisions, devoted to enrichment and invention. This is followed by a third period of timing and fine-tuning or polishing. This period culminates with the assimilation of all the technical facilities. The fourth and final period is the one in which the iris of the spotlight of the ensemble's collective attention is again opened wide to take in the whole. It is in this phase that the cast makes that all-important step from rehearsing to performing. That step that, in some plays, never happens at all or happens sometime during the run of the show. Actors in a well-directed and well-tuned production will find themselves shifting to a performance attitude during the last few rehearsals. It would be a psychological and semantic boost for actors if we could change the name of the *final dress rehearsal* to *final pre-performance*.

Some directors publish a rehearsal schedule on which a specific objective is spelled out for every rehearsal: Monday, Act I blocking; Tuesday, Act I motivations; Wednesday, Act I character development, etc. This, or course, has the clear advantage of focusing the cast's attention on a specific function for each rehearsal. However, it can have the disadvantage of encouraging fragmented and compartmentalized thinking which can hobble creativity. We believe that it is generally more productive to conduct rehearsals in terms of the gestalt, consciously striving to keep a sense of the whole, even – or especially – when focusing on details. Blocking, for instance, is generally learned more quickly if it is handled in terms of motivation and as a function of character development rather than as a mechanical function to be incorporated into the whole at some later date.

In any case, it is necessary that you publish a rehearsal schedule as early as possible – preferably before tryouts so that every actor is fully aware of his or her commitment. A typical schedule is illustrated in Figure 5, page 36. There is some advantage in laying out the schedule in the calendar-like foremat. It is very easy to read at a glance; it leaves some space for deletions, corrections or notations; and it lays out the entire rehearsal period in a graphic way so that the relation of any given rehearsal to opening night is ever evident.

Your own rehearsal schedule will, of course, reflect the specifics of your own situation, but an examination of the sample schedule will reveal some guiding principles that help in making decisions about the allocation of rehearsal time. Notice that each act and each scene is given almost exactly the same amount of rehearsal time. Beware of the pitfall of a schedule that over-budgets time for the first act and leaves the final scenes woefully neglected!

Observe also that once a section of the play has been blocked, it is never skipped for more than two rehearsal days. To allow any section to "lie fallow" for a longer period usually means spending extra time for the cast to "rediscover" the old material.

This schedule is based on a five day week, with all but the final weekend free. In educational theatre such a schedule is often dictated by the prevailing circumstances. You may well find yourself in a situation in which the seeming luxury of free weekends sounds unthinkable. Of course, as in any kind of theatre, you do what you have to do to get the show on! However, it is worth remembering that it can be very productive to build some regular days off into your schedule. Both you and your actors can profit by periodic breaks to step back and get perspective on the preceding week's work. Also, in amateur theatre your actors are all involved in a more or less complex juggling act, balancing their theatre commitment with their obligations to work, study and personal lives.

The Friday rehearsal that precedes the day or days off should pointedly

Figure 5   All calls 7 – 9:30 onstage
unless otherwise noted!

Rehearsal Schedule – TRAPPED BY A TREACHEROUS TWIN – (subject to change)

SUNDAY	MONDAY	TUESDAY	WEDNESDAY	THURSDAY	FRIDAY	SATURDAY
	Oct. 4 FULL COMPANY READ-THROUGH	Oct. 5 BLOCK & WORK I–1, pgs. 5 – 15 BRING PENCILS TO ALL REHEARSALS!	Oct. 6 I–1 Block I–1, pgs. 16 – 28 Run I–1	Oct. 7 Block I–2	Oct. 8 Review work on all of Act I	Oct. 9
Oct. 10 Off	Oct. 11 Block II–1	Oct. 12 Block II–2 and work all of Act II	Oct. 13 Work through all of Act I	Oct. 14 Work through all of Act II	Oct. 15 Work through entire play	Oct. 16 Off
Oct. 17 Off	Oct. 18 Work I–1 (Off Book!)	Oct. 19 Work I – 1 & 2 (Off Book!)	Oct. 20 Work II – 1	Oct. 21 Work II – 1 & 2	Oct. 22 Work through entire play	Off
Oct. 24 Off	Oct. 25 Work II–1 (Off Book!) Olio rehearsal Music rm. 7:30	Oct. 26 Work II–2 (Off Book!) Olios – Music rm. 7:30	Oct. 27 Work Act I Olios – Music rm. 7:30	Oct. 28 Work Act II Olios – Music rm. 7:30	Oct. 29 Work through I and II Olios – Mus. rm. 7:30	Oct. 30 Off
Oct. 31 Off	Nov. 1 Work through Olios – Music rm. 7:30	Nov. 2 Work through Olios – Music rm. 7:30	Nov. 3 RUN THROUGH INC. OLIOS! PUBLICITY PHOTOS ONSTAGE 6:00	Nov. 4 RUN THROUGH INCLUDING OLIOS Note: All remaining rehearsals will last until 10:30!	Nov. 5 RUN THROUGH	Nov. 6 Keep day open for special work if needed
Nov. 7 Off	Nov. 8 RUNTHROUGH WITH OLIOS AND M/C	Nov. 9 RUNTHROUGH WITH OLIOS AND M/C	Nov. 10 Preview Scenes for Assembly – 5th period Complete Runthrough 7:00	Nov. 11 RUN THROUGH WITH OLIOS AND M/C	Nov. 12 RUN THROUGH WITH OLIOS AND M/C	Nov. 13 TECH. REH. 2–7 PM
Nov. 14 First DRESS and MAKEUP SIGN IN BY 6 PM	Nov. 15 FULL DRESS REH. 6:00 CALL	Nov. 16 FINAL DRESS 6:00 CALL	Nov. 17 O P E N I N G!! 6:30 Call 8:00 Curtain	Nov. 18 PERFORMANCE	Nov. 19 PERFORMANCE	Nov. 20 FINAL PERF.

36

recap the work of the preceding week. It would, for example, be inefficient and counterproductive to block a new section of the play on a Friday and then leave it for two days. In fact, it is generally quite inefficient to block a section without allowing time to run it during the same rehearsal and to review it and rework it the very next day. In the sample schedule, the second rehearsal is devoted to blocking the first ten pages of the first scene. That is a relatively short section to block and you may well find that you can comfortably get through more than ten pages. The important thing is to always leave enough time at the end of any blocking rehearsal to run the new blocking at least once and preferably twice.

The question of when to call for line memorization is a perennial problem for directors. A premature call of an "off-book" rehearsal can trigger a devastating disintegration of everything that has been accomplished in previous rehearsals. A delayed call for lines is likely to result in a dangerously abbreviated period of polish and fine tuning. A good case can be made for those directors who elect to avoid designating any specific deadline for memorization. By conducting rehearsals in such a way that the script in the actor's hand becomes more of a frustrating impediment than a comforting crutch, the actor's own motivation is likely to result in his putting the script down at the earliest possible moment — usually sooner than you might have required on the published schedule!

We should point out, too, that the schedule shown in Figure 5 applies to a situation in which the olio acts are under the direction of a musical director and are being done by performers who are not members of the melodrama cast. That arrangement has the obvious advantage of allowing concurrent rehearsals for olios and the melodrama. If, as is frequently the case, the olios are being prepared by regular cast members, they must be worked on outside the scheduled rehearsal times. Unless your cast is unusually mature and experienced, it is probably a good idea to let them concentrate on performing their roles and give the olio experience to others. In any case, the olios should be integrated into the rehearsal run-throughs at least one week, preferably two weeks, before opening.

Some kinds of drama pose a legitimate need for extensive rehearsal discussions — rehearsals that can effectively take place with the cast seated around a table. Melodrama simply does not lend itself to that kind of approach. Because melodrama is essentially a physicalized conflict between easily recognized forces of good and evil, it is generally more productive to let the actors get on their feet and concentrate on finding effective ways to physicalize their story. Once the actors have an understanding of the "rules of the game of melodrama," they should be encouraged to work on relatively large segments of the play at any given rehearsal and to get to run-throughs as early in the rehearsal process as possible.

Early and frequent run-throughs can be effective and exciting if everyone concerned approaches each one with a real objective of constructive progress. A run-through that is nothing more than a rote repetition of yesterday's run-through can quickly become dull and counterproductive. Each rehearsal should be a process of growth and new discoveries. There is an interesting distinction between the words *practice* and *rehearse*. Practice has the connotation of a repetitive process of "going through it again." The word comes from the Greek word *practikos* meaning "to do." The word *rehearse* has its origins in an old French word *herce* which was an agricultural implement like a harrow used to dig through the soil. To rehearse, then, is to "dig through the material again," to re-explore and investigate. With this semantic "hair-splitting" in mind, it is obviously better to hold rehearsals than to have play practice.

D. Rehearsals

Of the thirty or so rehearsals you and your cast will devote to the preparation of your melodrama, none will be more important than the first one. It is traditional and appropriate that the cast read through the entire play at this rehearsal. Even more important than that reading, however, is your presentation in which you sketch the ground rules for melodrama, set the tone for the production and help the cast to arrive at a reasonably unified view of the entire project. The cast should leave the first rehearsal with a fairly clear idea of what kind of world they will be creating on the stage by opening night.

If you have sketches or renderings which depict the ultimate appearance of sets and costumes, they should be shared with the cast at this time. If melodrama is a new experience for any or all of your cast members, some background information is definitely in order. Pictures of other successful melodrama productions can be valuable aids for your actors.

That subtle blending of pathos and farce that modern melodrama audiences find so delightful is not an easy mark to hit. If the cast approaches the task as though their mission were to be corny and as outrageously funny as possible, the whole enterprise will almost certainly fall into a shambles of awkward and self-defeating silliness. Such misguided zeal generally produces little more than mutual embarrassment on both sides of the footlights! On the other hand, if the element of exaggeration and farce is neglected, the result can be downright boring.

Like any other kind of theatre, melodrama must establish a solid foundation of reality and truth. Melodrama's foundation, however, is not the reality and truth of the world as it is, was, or ought to be. It is the reality and truth of the world *as it might have been depicted on a stage a century ago*! It is a theatrical reality — a reality once removed.

It can be a very practical point of departure for the cast of a melodrama to view their undertaking as a kind of "theatre within a theatre." Let them imagine that they are to be playing the parts of nineteenth-century actors who are playing the roles of hero, heroine, villain, etc. The nineteenth-century actors can be absolutely serious in playing the authentic but heightened emotions of their characters.

Historically, of course, no nineteenth-century actor deliberately set out to be corny or outrageous in his performance. The prevailing style of acting was different than that of our own era. Most acting of the period was based on or influenced by the teachings of a French elocutionist named Francois Delsarte (1811 – 1871). Delsarte taught that "gesture was the agent of the soul." He developed and codified a system of movement and postures which were used to depict emotional and mental states. This system had a profound influence on acting from its introduction in 1839 until near the end of the century when the mannered and presentational style began to yield to the more subtle representational style of the new realism. Gestures, not necessarily Delsarte's, are in fact the agent of the soul of melodrama.

It will be a very good investment of time to devote the first few minutes of each rehearsal to helping the cast become familiar and comfortable with the exaggerated gestures and the broad, sweeping movements that are such an intrinsic part of the texture of melodrama. In order to play the parts of nineteenth-century actors playing melodrama characters, your cast will need to develop a sense of the physical language of the stage of that period.

In the realistic theatre of today, we are accustomed to highly representational drama which strives to create the "illusion of the first time." In effect, we try to make the audience forget that they are in a theatre. Toward that end, we cultivate the illusion of the "fourth wall" — that invisible esthetic buffer that separates the characters from the audience. Melodrama is more presentational than representational and the fourth wall simply does not exist. We don't want the audience to forget they are in a theatre. In fact, we go out of our way to remind them that they are in an old-fashioned theatre, participating in an old-fashioned play.

It is actually the elimination of that fourth wall that accounts for many of the significant differences between acting in a melodrama and in a modern, realistic play. Actors who are trained to work behind the fourth wall almost instinctively avoid the full-front body position — the stance in which the actor/character faces directly toward the audience. In melodrama, the full-front body position is the rule rather than the exception. The melodrama actor instinctively avoids profile position. Even while executing a horizontal cross, parallel to the footlights, the face and upper torso tend to open out toward the audience.

Actors may find this manner of walking strange at first, but with a little practice it can begin to feel like a perfectly natural means of getting from point A to point B! The feeling of the movement is as though the actor has a powerful magnet imbedded in the tip of the nose and the center of the chest. Those magnets exert a constant force toward the audience. Once the actor is comfortable with that idea, the foundation for appropriate period movement is established.

Gestures in melodrama are broad, open and pointed. It would be difficult to describe melodramas or melodramatic acting without the word *very*. Characters are *very* good or *very* bad. They tend to be *very* troubled or *very* happy or *very* frightened. Inarticulate understatements have no place in the melodramatic scheme of things. Vague or non-committal gestures are totally alien to the melodramatic style. If, in a moment of triumph, the heroine is going to point to the door to send the villain packing, she is going to do it with a flair that is *very* specific. No shrugging jerk of the head and jab of the thumb toward the door for her! Her gesture is going to leave absolutely no doubt in the mind of the villain or the audience. It will be a *very* elegant gesture with a crisp beginning, an eventful middle, and a theatrical end. Of course, it will be made with the upstage hand — those magnets in the nose and chest would not allow otherwise. The gesture will likely begin from a position about waist high.

(The energy and exuberance of melodrama seldom allow a character's hands to dangle at the sides.) Depending on the circumstances, the gesture will begin either just before or on the accompanying line of dialogue. Its initial impetus will seem to come from the shoulder as the hand, slightly trailing the wrist, inscribes a vertical arc in front of the actress' torso. At the top of the arc, the arm will straighten in a magnificent extension. That extended arm, index finger pointing rigidly toward the door, will hold for the duration of the speech and normally about three beats beyond it. During the life of that extended gesture, the full force of the heroine's indignation will gather as energy rising from the very soles of her feet, move through her body, and flow along that extended arm until it seems to erupt through the tip of the pointing index finger. When the moment is completed, the actress will redirect her energies to support the character's next action. The gesture will, in effect, retrace its course as the hand returns to its comfortable waist-high position.

Your cast members should spend a few minutes of drill at the beginning of each rehearsal experimenting with such grandly articulate gestures. They could each rehearse the pointing gesture described above, adapting it to suit the personality of their specific characters. Most actors have to relearn to use the joint at the shoulder. In our daily lives, many of us develop an unconscious reluctance to allow our elbows to get very far away from our rib cages. The result is that most of our gestures use only the forearm. In melodrama, gestures are larger than life-sized and are made with the entire arm, not just half of it.

There are a number of traditional gestures that the cast should add to their repertoire. The troubled heroine's "Oh, woe is me!" gesture of bringing the back of the hand to the brow is typically melodramatic. Like all gestures, it should be executed with a flair. Care must be taken to keep the elbow high and the forearm almost parallel to the floor so that the gesture does not conceal the face from the audience. When suddenly smitten by love, the hands go to cover the heart gently, as though to muffle the pounding. The heroine will generally perform that gesture with both hands while the hero, equally susceptible to Cupid's arrows, will only use one hand for the gesture.

The *aside* is a theatrical convention which dates back to the ancients. It has been used to one degree or another in every theatrical era except our own. It fell into disfavor with the advent of twentieth-century realism. It is so frequently associated with melodrama that it is often considered almost a melodrama trademark. It is nothing more than a speech, usually a very short one, addressed to the audience and by mutual agreement not heard by other characters on the stage. It is a valuable tool for the melodrama actor because, almost without exception, an aside is calculated to generate an audible audience response. Some actors get timid with the aside and deliver the lines at half volume. The reverse should be true. All dialogue in a melodrama should be slightly over-projected and asides should be a bit louder — not softer — than the surrounding lines. The aside is usually delivered as the actor takes a small step toward the audience. The original tradition called for asides to be delivered with the actor's hand beside the mouth, as though to prevent the others from overhearing. Some directors continue to use this convention for all asides. Others feel that the hand-by-the-mouth gesture is so often associated with the villain that they reserve it just for him. Other characters step forward for the aside, but rely on tone and expression to make it clear that the words are meant only for the audience.

One caution about the use of asides is in order and should be relayed to your cast long before opening. Asides are *always* delivered *in character*. We have seen too many situations in which an actor, carried away by the lively response of the audience, suddenly ad libs comments back to the audience, speaking as the *actor* and not as the *character*. Such an action inevitably shatters the illusion of old-fashioned theatre and plunges the performance into instant trouble. Sometimes, with a particularly animated audience, the temptation to try some ad libbed asides can be very great. That is a temptation that should be resisted at all costs! If it simply can not be resisted, be sure that it is the *character* who makes the comment.

The simple fact is that in melodrama as in most other kinds of theatre, the actors' ultimate objective — the very reason for all those rehearsals — is to transform *self* into *character*. The audience comes to see the *characters*, not the *actors*. In that sense, anything that reveals the *actor* on the stage defeats the purpose of the production! The cast of a melodrama has, as we have pointed out, two roles to play: they must become the nineteenth-century cast playing the playwright's characters. The style and technique — the grand manner of melodrama — all exist for the single purpose of creating that nineteenth-century cast. Those early actors were deadly serious about creating their roles. Today's actors must be equally serious about creating both their actor roles and their character roles. Any effort to lampoon or burlesque the style will fail automatically *because it allows the performer to come between the character and the audience*!

Because of the cultural change from the last century to this one, the material will parody itself if it is presented honestly and simply. The audience will respond to the parody with delight. However, if the performers get in the way by seeming to approach the audience with a "Hey, look how funny we are!" attitude, the parody is aborted and both the performers and the audience will find themselves in for a very long evening.

E. Groaners, Gags and Gimmicks

While any attempts to burlesque melodramatic material or to embellish it with funny business that lacks any basis in character or situation are doomed to fail, the exploration of the legitimate comic potential is a vital part of the rehearsal process. The basic appeal of melodrama lies in its invitation to the audience to become participants — to hiss and boo the villain's treachery, to cheer the hero's valiant deeds, and to loudly lament the heroine's plight. The director's responsibility includes the careful charting of the nature and frequency of specific invitations to the audience to respond. With the possible exception of intricate passages of exposition requiring intense audience attention, audible audience reactions ought to happen on a fairly regular basis. While there is no exact formula for programming cheers, boos and laughter, a reasonable rule of thumb is to try to trigger something from the audience at least once for each page of dialogue or about once every two minutes. If you find that five or more minutes of playing time is passing without some kind of "hook" to grab an audience's audible reaction, you had better invent something that will do the trick.

That need for arbitrary invention is the pitfall that lures some melodrama directors to disaster. Be careful to resist the temptation to indulge in what we call "wearing the lampshade," which is doing something that you hope will be funny just because it is ridiculous — being funny just for the sake of being funny. The litmus paper test for a piece of business is *does it enhance or dramatize the situation and is it something that the character(s) would say or do*? For instance, if the heroine's plight has reduced her to tears, it would be legitimate to attempt to involve the audience in the process. It might be a real rehearsal crack-up for the cast if, in her misery, she wailed like a banshee and blew her nose on the window curtains — but it would turn the audience off because it is totally out of character. (It would be a case of the actress trying to be funny!) If you want the audience to join in with compassionate ooo's and aaaah's, have the actress conceal a wet sponge in her handkerchief. After she dries her eyes, let her wring out the hidden sponge so that the audience sees the small stream of water fall to the floor. That is a very broad piece of comic business, but it will work like a charm because it is consistent with character and dramatizes the situation. Actually, such a piece of business not only dramatizes, it *melodramatizes* the situation. After all, that *is* the name of the game!

Bits of business that melodramatize can be quite broad — even to the point of being outrageous — as long as they pass the test of fidelity to character and situation. The more outrageous the business, the more deadpan and sincere the actor must be in executing it. If the sheriff has finally captured the villain and is holding him at gunpoint with a line such as, "Don't move or I'll blow your brains out!" it can be genuinely funny if, seemingly by accident, the gun, at that exact moment, happens to be pointing at the villain's posterior instead of his head. The gag will not work, however, if the actor playing the sheriff tries to be cute about it or if the execution is studied, deliberate or obvious.

Audiences love to answer rhetorical questions. Latter-day authors of old-fashioned melodramas frequently build in "hooks" for audience response by using rhetorical questions as asides. The heroine, confused by a sweet-talking villain, may well have an aside such as, "Dare I trust his honied words?" If the question is played sincerely and simply, you can count on audible and laudible advice from an enthusiastic audience. If your playwright has neglected to pose that question, it is within the bounds of melodrama ethics to have your heroine add it as an ad lib.

Because melodramas deal in stock characters and stock situations, you soon discover that there are many gags and gimmicks that are interchangeable from play to play. The more fiendish the villain, the more delight the audience takes in his comeuppance. If, as is so often the case, he is floored by a timely blow to the chin delivered by the hero, it is only justice that you allow the audience plenty of time to enjoy it. Let the hero deliver the blow, but then stop the action as the villain remains standing! If the villain seems glassy-eyed and quite literally "out on his feet," the audience can have plenty of time to cheer before the hero tops the gag with a snap of his fingers or a gentle touch with his forefinger which sends the villain crashing belatedly to the floor! Such split action is appropriate in many melodramas and is a valuable tool because it gives the audience two occasions to cheer (the blow and the fall) instead of just one.

Let us emphasize again that gags such as the delayed fall may strain credulity but they must not break it. In this case, it is legitimate because it is a plausible product of the director's perennial game of "what if?" *What if* the hero's blow stunned the villain who remained on his feet through the power of unconscious malicious stubbornness? The hero's *coup de grace* can then be accepted as a logical extension of that premise.

There is a world of difference between the necessary director's game of "what if?" and the very dangerous game of "why not?" The "why not?" directorial attitude can too easily lose touch with the disciplined adherence to the limits of credibility. "What if?" however, begins with a plausible premise. As long as that clause of plausibility is observed, your latitude for directorial invention is as broad as melodrama itself.

Audiences also enjoy having their illusion of being in an old-fashioned theatre by little planned suggestions that things are not always perfect backstage. For instance, in *Little Orphan Angela*, early in Act II, the heroine, Angela, has the following speech. " . . . Hark! Do I hear a knock? (There is a knock.) I hear a knock! Who could this be? (She crosses to the door.)" The line preceding the sound gets a laugh because it allows the audience to feel that some unknown backstage helper has been caught "asleep at the switch." In this case, it is vitally important that the actress stay in character — or specifically her *double* character as the nineteenth-century actress playing the role of the heroine. If she lapses from either of those characters or "mugs" to try to make a big thing of it, the laugh will either not be forthcoming or worse, it will be at the personal expense of the actress. In either case, the illusion of old-time theatrical reality will be broken. It is frequently a long, uphill struggle to win back the audience after such a mishap.

F. Special Effects

Melodrama productions should resist any temptation to get technically sophisticated with the creation of special effects. Theatre of the late nineteenth century actually was showing great ingenuity in creating astounding illusions of enormous complexity — but that is *not* the theatre that is the "patron saint" of modern melodrama productions. The spirit of modern melodramas has its roots in the naive simplicity of a provincial road company following the railroad to villages, farm centers and mining camps all across the land. That is the reason that throughout this book we have repeatedly urged you to err on the side of simplicity.

Even if your theatre is equipped with the very latest in high fidelity sound equipment, for example, you probably would not make much use of it in your melodrama production. The sound of approaching horses on a professional quality commercial sound effects record played over an expensive sound system would not be as appropriate or effective as the sound of two empty coconut shells drumming against a pine board in the wings.

Inclement weather seems to be a prevailing condition in melodramas! Practically no self-respecting melodrama can get by for long without a violent storm of some sort. That means that a good *wind machine* should be a priority item in any melodrama theatre. A very effective one can be made in the shop out of mostly scrap materials. A wind machine is merely a hand-cranked wooden drum over which is draped a piece of tent-quality heavy canvas. The drum should be approximately twenty-four to thirty inches in diameter and thirty to thirty-six inches long. It is made by starting with round wooden pieces to serve as the ends of the drum. These are held together by a series of one inch by one inch sticks fastened around the circumference of the ends at intervals of every three or four inches. It is the friction of these sticks or ribs rubbing against the canvas cover when the drum is rotated that creates a very satisfactory sound of wind. With no more than a few minutes of practice, any operator can simulate a very authentic sounding wind storm. Every old-time theatre had just such an instrument which would have been used to create the wind sound in the original old-time melodramas. (See illustration, Figure 6, page 47.)

The *thunder sheet* is another standard piece of homemade equipment that no melodrama theatre should be without. It is a large sheet of tin or other thin metal. The metal should be at least three feet by eight feet. It is sandwiched at the top and bottom with wooden slats. It is rigged to hang freely from overhead, and the bottom cleats have a handle attached. This simple device produces a very realistic thunder effect when it is rippled and an effective crack of thunder wnen its bottom is snapped sharply. (See illustration, Figure 7, page 48.) Like the wind machine, the thunder sheet is much more effective than the most sophisticated electronically produced sound.

Figure 6

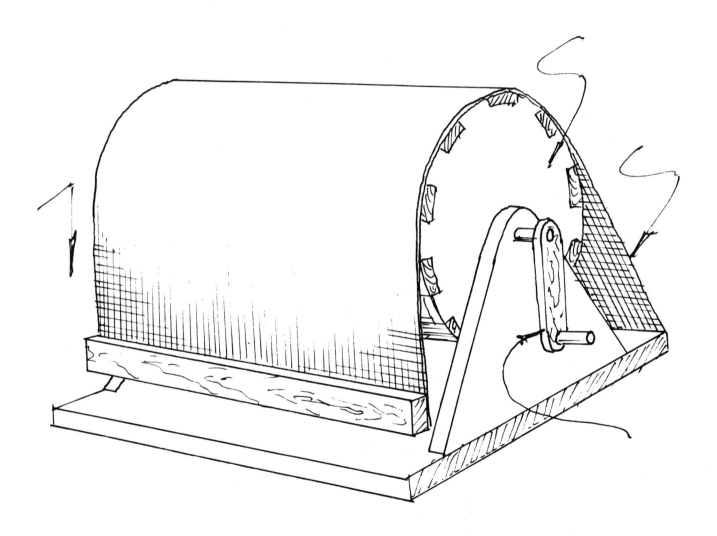

WIND MACHINE

Figure 7

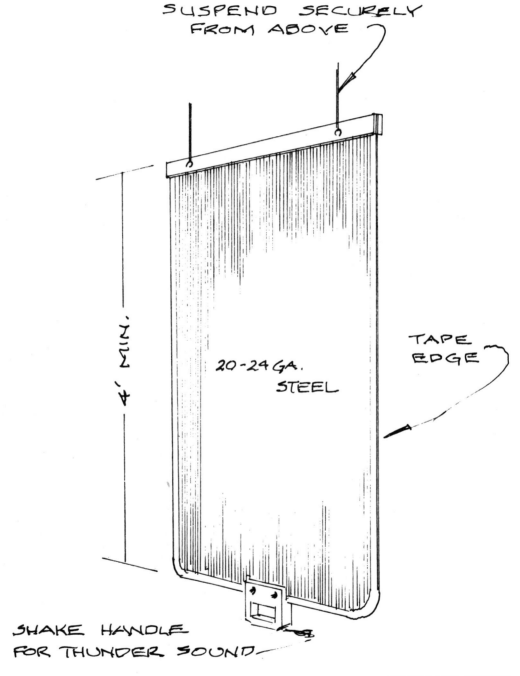

SUSPEND SECURELY FROM ABOVE

4' MIN.

20-24 GA. STEEL

TAPE EDGE

SHAKE HANDLE FOR THUNDER SOUND

THUNDER SHEET

Along with wind and thunder comes the deluge of rain! The sound of rain is another effect that is best produced by a simple, homemade device. The *rain machine* is very similar in appearance to the wind machine. It is a hollow drum three or four feet in diameter and about one foot wide. (See illustration, Figure 8, page 50.) Strips of wood are fastened to the inside surface of the drum at intervals of five or six inches. This cylinder is equipped with an axle of pipe and mounted on a frame which will allow it to rotate freely. Two or three cups of dried peas are put into the cylinder through an access door in one end. When the cylinder is turned, the slats pick up the peas, carry them to the top, and allow them to drop to the bottom. This action creates a very good sound effect of rain. The quality of the sound can be varied by substituting dried beans or various sized buckshot for the peas. Volume of sound can be modified by altering the speed with which the drum is rotated. A little experimentation will produce the sound that exactly fits the specific situation.

In the world of melodrama, it is more likely to snow than to rain. The visual effect of snow seen through a door or window is often an important element in a melodrama production. This is another effect that is readily achieved with a simple handmade device. (See illustration, Figure 9, page 51.) The *snow dispenser* is a long shallow box, approximately eight to ten inches wide and deep and long enough to extend somewhat beyond the expanse of the door or window through which the falling snow is to be seen. The bottom of this box or trough is wire screen. The size of the mesh or openings in the screen will depend on the selection of material used as snow. The box is suspended above the door or window on dual lines rigged in such a way that it can be easily rocked by pulling on lines from the floor.

The most authentic looking substance to use for snow is regular theatrical snow used in the movie and television studios. This substance, a specially shredded plastic material, is available from any of the Hollywood theatrical supply houses. It is the most effective, but by no means the least expensive "snow" available. If this material is used, the screen at the bottom of the box should have a mesh of approximately one-half inch openings. Because of the expense involved, it is a good idea to lay out a sheet of clean muslin on the floor to catch the snow so that it can be easily collected and reused. When the snow box is in position, a loose muslin cradle should be positioned under it to prevent any "unseasonable" or unwanted snowfall. This cradle should be rigged in such a way that it can be easily removed when the snowfall is wanted.

Figure 8

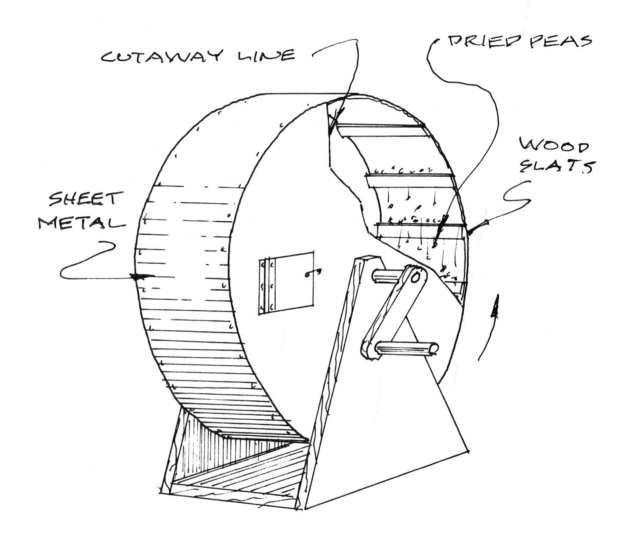

CUTAWAY LINE

DRIED PEAS

WOOD SLATS

SHEET METAL

RAIN MACHINE

Figure 9

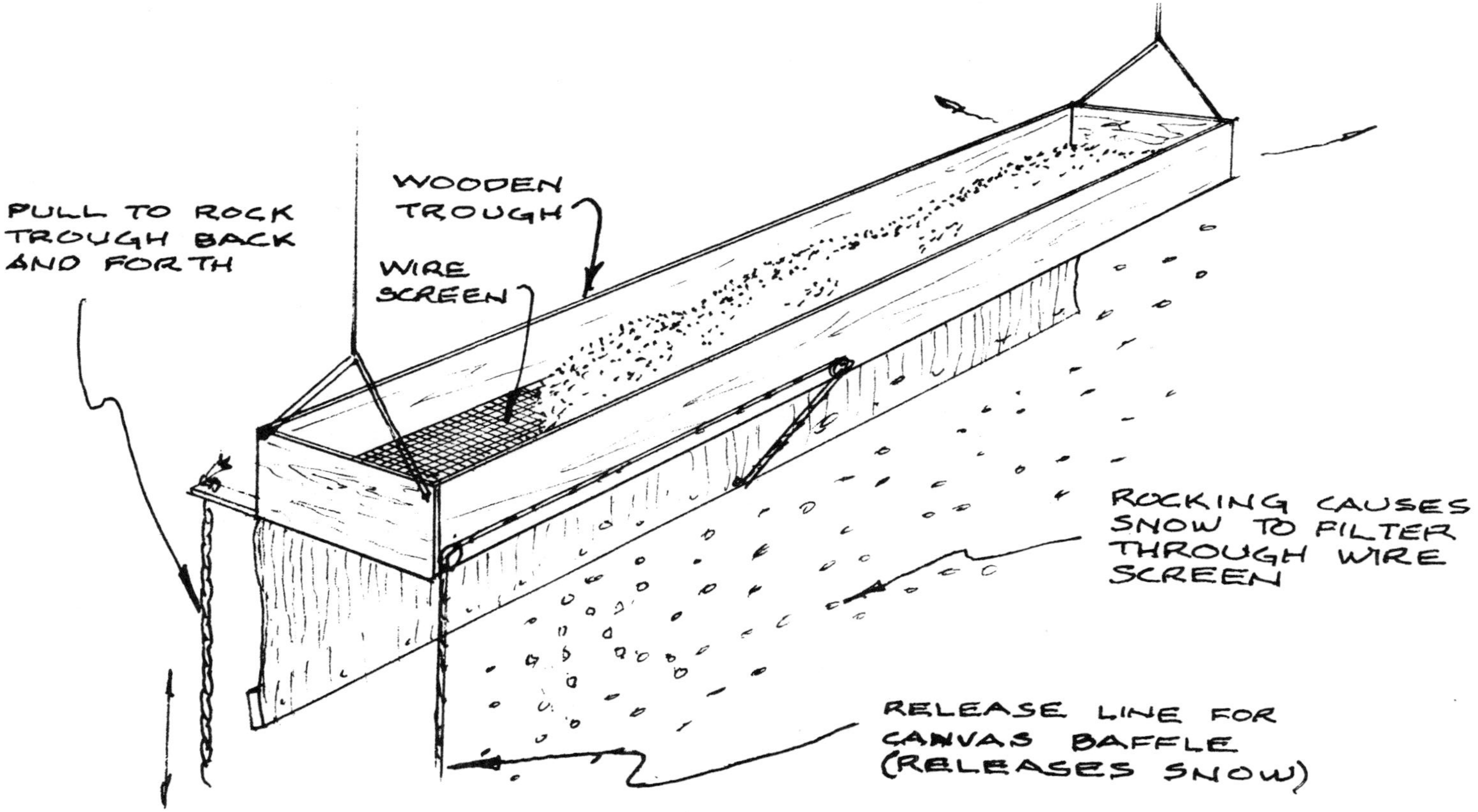

PULL TO ROCK TROUGH BACK AND FORTH

WOODEN TROUGH

WIRE SCREEN

ROCKING CAUSES SNOW TO FILTER THROUGH WIRE SCREEN

RELEASE LINE FOR CANVAS BAFFLE (RELEASES SNOW)

SNOW MACHINE

Gypsum is much less expensive and makes a satisfactory snow. Gypsum is normally available from agricultural supply houses. Other practical substitutes include coarsely ground salt, pulverized styrofoam, or finely shredded paper. Some experimentation will be needed to determine the best material for your use, and the most effective size openings in the screened bottom of the snow box.

Melodramas often build suspense in highly effective and theatrical moments by the use of the sound of a squeaking or creaking door. The sound effects department of every old-time theatre included a marvelously simple device called the *bull roarer* for this purpose. (See illustration, Figure 10, page 53.) The bull roarer is simply a large tin can mounted, bottom up, to a board. The bottom of the can has a small hole through which is fed a length of wire or sash cord, knotted on the inside so that it may be pulled taut. To operate this remarkable device, hold the wire or cord tight and rub it with a cloth treated with powdered rosin. The quality and pitch of the resulting sound will vary with the degree of tension with which the cord is held, as well as with the size of the can used and the texture of line or wire. A little experimentation will demonstrate the versatility of this simple instrument.

A word of caution should be added with regard to the use of firearms on the stage. Guns equipped to fire blank cartridges are, by no means, harmless toys. They must be handled on the stage with precisely the same respect due a gun loaded with live ammunition. Such a gun actually discharges wadding from the shell and that wadding becomes a missile capable of inflicting a painful injury. Should such a missile strike an actor in the eye, the consequences would be serious indeed! Obviously a stage gun loaded with blanks should *never* be fired at point-blank range at another actor or toward the audience! Any scene involving the discharge of a blank gun onstage must be rehearsed with choreographic precision to assure fail-safe control. The gun should be carefully aimed upstage of the "victim," and toward the floor.

Because of the risks involved, we urgently recommend that live blanks be the absolutely last resort in solving the problem of onstage shots. The very nature of melodrama's "reality once removed" gives the director a much wider range of options than might be acceptable in other theatrical styles. The very charm of the theatrical world of melodrama makes it quite appropriate to have the shots fired from a "cover gun" in the wings. With a bit of rehearsal care, coordination of the shot with the onstage business can be quite reliable. If the

Figure 10

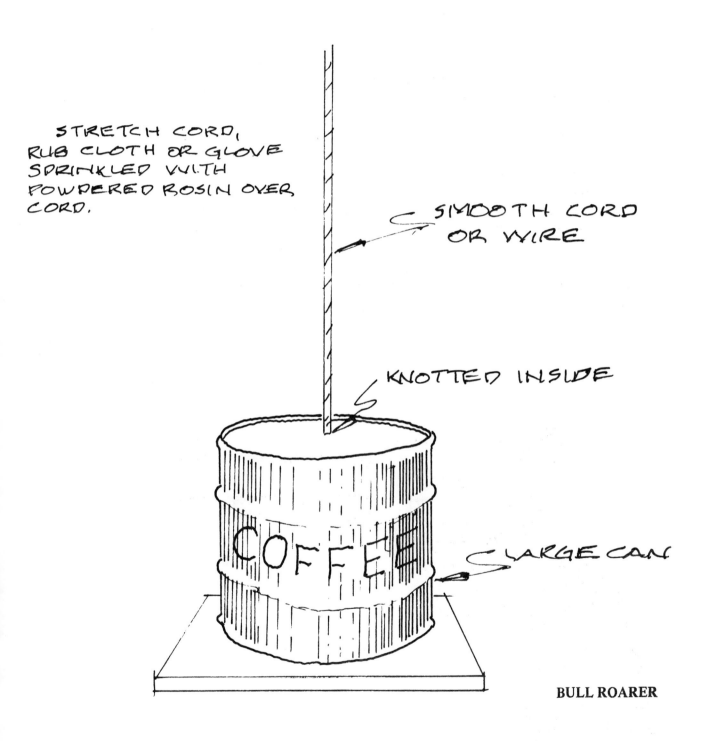

STRETCH CORD,
RUB CLOTH OR GLOVE
SPRINKLED WITH
POWDERED ROSIN OVER
CORD.

SMOOTH CORD
OR WIRE

KNOTTED INSIDE

COFFEE

LARGE CAN

BULL ROARER

53

audience, however, perceives imperfection in the coordination, so much the better! That is part of the charm that makes melodrama so much fun for audiences! For this very reason, even the offstage sound seldom demands shooting actual blanks.

A very effective gun shot sound can be produced with a simple slap-stick struck sharply against a flat surface. In the premiere production of the authors' melodrama, *Showdown at the Rainbow Ranch*, the problem of two closely spaced shots was solved delightfully by just such a device. Even though the moment comes at the very climax of the show, the fact that it was deliberately obvious to the audience that the shots were produced from offstage added to the effectiveness and the audience's enjoyment of the moment.

It is very easy to improvise a slap-stick which is simply two long boards fastened together in such a way that they slap together loudly when they are struck against a surface. In the tradition of the Commedia Dell' Arte players, that surface was another actor's posterior. However, a little experimenting, we're sure, will reveal more satisfactory surfaces.

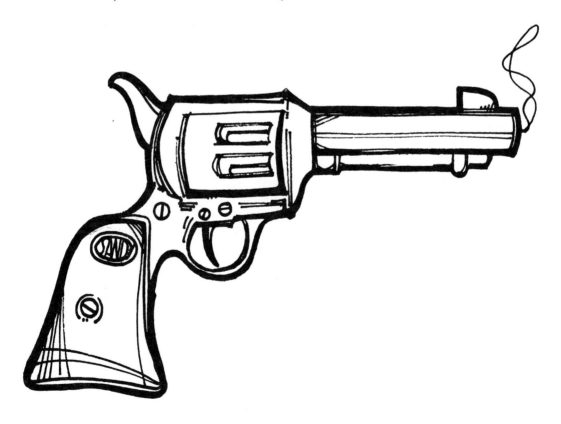

CHAPTER II

To The Actor

Making Tryouts Less Trying

With few exceptions, actors view auditions with feelings that range from discomfort to dire panic. If it is any comfort, remember that your misgivings place you in the company of most of the world's distinguished actors. By the way, it wouldn't hurt to realize that most directors share a dread of the process. However, we just have to get used to the idea that tryouts are a fact of theatrical life. If you wish to be an actor, either as a hobby or as a profession, it is an urgent necessity that you become a good auditioner.

Tryouts are a process in which the director seeks to screen candidates in order to assemble the very best available cast. It is not a popularity contest! Your job at tryouts is to demonstrate that you have the potential to become a valuable member of the cast and that you are genuinely committed to the prospect.

Your most valuable asset in this effort is *preparation*. In most academic situations, the script will be available for some time before tryouts. If it is, move heaven and earth to arm yourself with a copy as early as possible. When you get the script, read it. Then read it again. Most actors agree that the first five things you do with a script is read it! When you go out for a part, it helps to have a clear picture of what it is that you wish to be a part of.

As you become thoroughly familiar with the play, encourage your imagination to visualize the characters. See them move. Hear them speak. In this process of visualization, which of the characters can you see yourself becoming? This is an important choice to make — and one that too many tryout candidates neglect entirely. Be sure your choice is made on the basis of qualities you feel you could project, rather than on the size of the role. Putting all your energies toward trying for the hero's part because it is the "juiciest" can be a costly mistake if your stature and quality make you better suited to play the friendly sheriff or the comic hired hand. In other words, try to identify with the role or roles for which you have the most to offer — not necessarily the ones that have the most to offer to you. This decision is always important and usually difficult. The poet Robert Burns could well have had actors in mind when he lamented that we lack the power to "see ourselves as others see us."

That power does not come easily for most of us, but the pursuit of it is a vital part of any actor's preparation. Visualizing yourself as the various characters is often a very helpful approach. If you are a newcomer to the process, don't hesitate to ask. After you have familiarized yourself with the play, there is nothing at all wrong with seeking out the director well in advance of tryouts and asking what part or parts it would be best for you to seek.

If you are lucky, you may see a part that has "you" written all over it. Usually, however, it is unwise to focus exclusively on a single part. Broaden your scope to include a second or third choice. When your choices are made, read the part or parts aloud as frequently as possible. At first, you may wish to try reading aloud in the privacy of your own room. A bit later it may be helpful to find another candidate willing to read scenes with you.

Remember that the preparation process is really just intended to equip you with maximum familiarity with the material. It is almost always a mistake to attempt an all-out performance at tryouts. Your goal is to demonstrate a potential — not to prove that you're ready to open tomorrow! Many directors are put off by flashy "performances" at tryouts because such performances have a way of being rehearsal proof. The overzealous actor tends to get locked into a preconceived way of playing and, consciously or unconsciously, resists the normal process of growth through rehearsals. Your aim at tryouts is to show potential, not an end product.

This requires the ability to read the material clearly, getting the words and the sense of the words off the page and out to the auditors. At the same time, you are attempting to show that you have an awareness of the *quality* of the character, a sense of the nature (style) of the production, and — perhaps most important of all — a stage presence. Stage presence is not easy to define, but essentially it is a quality that says, "I can comfortably command my space on the stage. I really belong here."

Tryouts come in many forms, ranging from open auditions to closed-door interviews. In any case, you are almost certain to be asked to read from the play. In the case of the open auditions, you will probably read with one or more other auditioners in front of the director and a sizeable gathering of other candidates. Your chance to show stage presence begins the moment you start toward the stage or reading area. If you are human, you will have a cargo of doubts, misgivings and apprehensions. Fold them neatly and leave them on your chair. Don't worry! They'll be waiting for you there when you finish.

The reading area is frequently a bare stage with inadequate rehearsal lights. If this is the case, you should have already noticed where the best light is. Head for that spot! You are there to be seen and heard so avoid lurking in the shadows. Having watched and listened to others who have preceded you, you undoubtedly will have seen "hiders." They are the ones who stay in the dark, hide their faces behind scripts, or turn away from their auditors so they can't be seen at all! Do not be a hider.

You are there to be seen and heard. When you read, read to be heard. You have seen the hiders and you have heard the mumblers. Don't emulate either. Reading aloud is a rather special talent and a vital one to the art of auditioning. It is a talent that can and must be developed by the aspiring actor. The kind of familiarization that we have suggested will make the job easier.

Some audition situations, however, offer little or no opportunity for such preparation. There are directors who prefer not to make scripts available before tryouts. If that is the case, you are stuck with the necessity of "cold" readings. These are probably the most difficult readings. Obviously the actor who has developed the knack of cold readings will have the edge. The best way to develop that knack is through practice. Practice cold reading for at least fifteen minutes every day. Either in private or to a volunteer listener, read aloud at random from any source for a few minutes every day. Read the evening newspaper, your biology text, or from plays — but read and read aloud. Regularly. It will eventually give you a distinct edge at cold readings.

Do not leave to chance your attire for the tryouts. Select your clothing and hair style with some care. The choice will depend to a degree on the character(s) for which you are auditioning. If you see yourself as a heroine, don't present yourself in blue jean cut-offs, sweat shirt and sandals with your hair in a pony tail! We are not suggesting that you show up in a costume from the 1890's! At this stage of the game, you are not trying to *be* the heroine; you are projecting an image of an actress who has the potential to play the heroine. To that end, a dress or a skirt and sweater would project a better image than jeans. If your face looks softer with your hair down, by all means wear it down. A word of caution, however: be careful that your hair doesn't hang in such a way that it keeps your audience from seeing your face. If you are trying out for Aunt Bessie and you look a little older with your hair up, wear it up.

It is a good idea to project the same appearance when you are called back to read again another day. This can reinforce the image you are trying to project — and if the director doesn't already know you well, it helps to identify you. Directors sometimes use clothing or hair style notes to single out an individual from among the dozens and dozens of others seen during the casting process. We have seen a situation, repeated many times, in which a director at call-backs may ask an aide, "Where's that blonde girl with the yellow sweater?" when the girl in question was seated not ten feet away, but this time she had her hair up under a kerchief and had all but disappeared in a bulky gray parka.

Of course, you do not want to make a nuisance of yourself, but you *do* want to let the director know that you are present — and interested! If you have read and have received no feedback, it is perfectly legitimate to approach the director at a convenient time with a request to be heard again. Put your request in a positive form. "I think that character has more energy and enthusiasm than I had in my reading. Could I read again to show you what I mean?" Such a request — tactfully phrased — lets the director know that you are serious in your efforts and flexible in your approach. If the director should give you any hints or suggestions about your reading, listen carefully and do your best to respond to the suggestions.

If you are asked to read for a role that you hadn't considered, don't panic. It may well be a signal that the director sees a quality in your reading that you didn't realize was there. Adjust to that situation as quickly and as intelligently as possible. Remember, too, that the director must keep in mind a myriad of production-wide considerations that may transcend the quality of your reading. You may be auditioning beautifully but not be a good physical or vocal mix with other finalists. The suggestions should also be seized upon as another boost in your effort to "see yourself as others see you."

CHAPTER III

To The Music Director

Just as the director must give careful consideration to the preparation of a script, so does the job of the music director begin with a thorough study of the play at hand. It is the music director who, answering only to the director, assumes responsibility for the selection and production of all music, incidental or fundamental, to be used in a show, both in rehearsal and during performances.

Because melody is such a basic ingredient of melodrama, the script should be rehearsed with music as soon as blocking has been completed. This gives both actors and accompanist(s) a smooth sense of timing.

The music director must determine well in advance of rehearsals the choice of music to be used and at which points throughout the play. There should, of course, always be opportunity during rehearsals to add to, subtract from, or otherwise improve upon the placement and timing of music in the same way that the director continues to shape and reshape the dramatic action. This is, after all, what rehearsals are all about!

The production of music in melodrama may be as modest or as elaborate as resources permit.

A piano, visible to the audience, most often provides accompaniment although it is, by no means, the only choice. For example, the original production of *Trapped by a Treacherous Twin* as staged by California State University Fresno featured piano as the primary instrument with violin and trumpet for emphasis. A more recent production of *Little Orphan Angela* by Detroit's Fine Arts Society added cello to the above.

The fact that incidental music is seldom cued into a script is no reason to take it for granted. The selection of this material can be as creative as the writing of a play itself, for these accompaniments are as intrinsic to melodrama as are butter and salt to popcorn!

A. Incidental Music

In order to better understand the function of incidental music in

59

melodrama, let's consider first the music of motion pictures. Until circa 1926, when a movie called *The Jazz Singer* changed the course of the film industry, silent movies were accompanied by live music provided by the theatres in which they were shown. If the theatre was a major one, there would be a full orchestra which played a complete score released by the studio which had produced the movie. Smaller theatres employed organists who had to rely on cue sheets for particular scenes, all but composing incidental music on the spot, often with little or no rehearsal. Imagine the ingenuity and creative talent required of the musician called upon to punctuate the action of a boat, a train, an airplane, a tidal wave, a fire, an explosion — sometimes all during a single performance!

As silent films gave way to "talkies," with their accompanying soundtracks, background music became more sophisticated. Motion picture music became a medium all its own. Can there be anyone — having seen *Gone With the Wind* — who could imagine this classic without the haunting *Tara's Theme*? Surely it is equally difficult to direct the mind's eye to *The Bridge on the River Kwai* without the mind's ear being filled with its now famous march music.

There is no doubt that thrillers or chillers, documentaries or cartoons, much of the magic of cinema derives directly from its music.

Incidental music is as elemental to television in general as it is to movies and, probably, the prime example of its importance within this medium is found in the television soap opera.

The daily "soaps," with their rapid production schedules and resulting lack of rehearsal time, must rely heavily on loosely-followed scripts and lots of accompanying music to accentuate action. Picture, for example, the lonely lover bent over the writing of a long letter. Viewing this scene in the absence of background music would be about as exciting as reading in the dark!

Even in the light of latter-day sound technology, a chase by auto or by helicopter is invariably more arousing when accompanied by appropriate music. This kind of incidental music is sometimes so adroitly composed and/or inserted as to go almost unnoticed by its audience. It is, nevertheless, critical to the final effect.

As we've said, melodramatic elements can be found in literally every period of theatrical history. As we see here, they continue to exist in many aspects of modern entertainment. Incidental music is not only basic to melodrama, it is a highly important element in the degree of success of any production.

A.1) Special Themes

Incidental music for melodrama may be divided into two categories. *Character Themes* are used under entrances and exits of principals. *Situation Themes* are interspersed throughout the drama to accent emotional moments.

Character themes should be carefully suited to the characters they represent. A "Villain's Theme," creepy and menacing, should be played for the villain and a contrasting passage of noble and stouthearted quality should accompany the hero. The heroine must, of course, have her own theme, typically innocent and sweet, as should all other major characters, comic or tragic. Familiar songs with names in their titles are often appropriate. Character themes are useful not only under entrances and exits as previously mentioned. They are often effective as reference to an offstage character. An example of this is our use of *The Farmer in the Dell* when referring to the gone-but-not-forgotten Farmer Tilford in *Little Orphan Angela*.

Situation themes are used to accent emotional moments indicating romance, joy, victory, trouble, tragedy, chase, and countless more sentiments deemed by the director and music director to be worthy of audience reaction. *I Love You Truly* and Tchaikowsky's love theme from *Romeo and Juliet* are popular choices for such romantic moments as when hero and heroine meet for the first time and for later when they vow their love for each other. Bizet's *Toreador Song* from *Carmen* works under many fights and *The Lone Ranger Theme* as based on Rossini's *William Tell Overture* makes good chase or off-to-the-rescue music. The victory theme from Beethoven's *Fifth Symphony* should be self-explanatory!

Some theme music must be categorized as somewhere between characters and situations. For instance, *My Bonnie* and *Row, Row, Row Your Boat*, both nautical in flavor, may be used to represent an individual or to refer to a situation. Likewise, themes which suggest locations such as *The Sidewalks of New York* or *My Old Kentucky Home* may be used to refer to those places or to characters coming from or going to them.

Still another effective use of incidental music in melodrama is the practice of replacing a line of dialogue with a line of music sung *a capella*. Take, for example, a common melodramatic exchange:

VILLAIN (to HEROINE). I ask you, for the last time, will you be mine?
HEROINE. No! Never!

This is easily changed so that the heroine answers in song:

HEROINE (singing). No! No! A thousand times, no! I'd rather die than say "Yes!"

Unlike some theatrical gimmicks which require repetition to be most effective, a little of this sort of thing goes a long way.

The audience loves the unexpected. We have played Beethoven's *Minuet in G* under a desperate struggle between hero and villain. In order for this kind of "foolishness" to work the action must be blocked in time to the music. The effect is a form of visual slow motion and we have yet to see it fail. Another example of this tongue-in-cheek approach is to play a lullaby or *Twinkle, Twinkle, Little Star* if the villain is knocked down!

It is often possible to achieve a particular effect of incidental music by repeating a previously established theme in a minor key to stress tragedy or disaster. We played *Home, Sweet Home* as the curtain opened on the Act I farmhouse kitchen scene in *Little Orphan Angela*. Then, in the Act II kitchen scene, after the death of the farmer, we played *Home, Sweet Home* in minor. The possibilities in this direction are practically limitless.

A.2) Use of Incidental Music

Equally important in the implementation of incidental music in melodrama as *what* to use is *when* to use it.

As much as a full chorus or more may be played at the opening or closing of a scene in order to establish a location or condition. This also works as a short bridge between scenes. By contrast, it takes only a few notes, just enough to make a melody recognizable, to identify a character or state a point in the dialogue. Usually, a few chords or bars of a song are enough to achieve any effect.

Lest it defeat its purpose, incidental music cannot be allowed to outplay the drama. Lines which seem to beg for musical emphasis may be followed by others which will be lost by the music which precedes them. Too much music, no matter how appropriate in content, interrupts the flow of the dialogue and is, therefore, distracting.

How much or how little incidental music to use at any one given time constitutes a careful decision on the part of the music director. Whereas too much may stall the action, too little can be a complete waste of time.

As we've said, incidental music is intended as emphasis and, as such, must be perfectly appropriate in order to work. At worst, this musical emphasis may be predictable, adequate, and basically forgettable. In the partnership of a director and music director working together with any degree of imagination, it can be memorable, extremely entertaining, and a high point of any production.

Some melodramas rely solely on incidental music while others, like musical comedy, contain a score of original musical numbers within the body of the script.

Still others integrate popular songs of the period into the play, either as suggested by the author or as inserted by the director. For instance, the old classic *Father, Dear Father, Come Home With Me Now!* by nineteenth-century songwriter Henry Clay Work has brought many a tear to many an eye as sung by Little Mary in *Ten Nights in a Barroom*. Today's still-popular *Home, Sweet Home* by J. H. Payne and H. R. Bishop made its debut in *The Drunkard*.

There are countless well-known songs of the Gay Nineties period with themes fitting into the plots of melodramas which do not have original music in their scripts.

A lengthy selection of Gay Nineties' music will be found in "The Melo(s) in Melodrama," section B of this chapter.

In such "musical" melodramas, particularly those which call for a chorus, we prefer to work with a vocal coach. As in the delivery of dialogue, breathing, phrasing, and enunciation are extremely important in the delivery of songs. Songs, unfortunately, seldom seem to come out of the mouths, especially collective ones, with automatic full-blown clarity! With a little more of that advance planning we so strongly advocate, most music rehearsals may take place while the play is being blocked or while other business is worked, thus making dual use of rehearsal time. Any extra time taken may be considered well spent.

Nineteenth-century melodrama was the drama of the people and its music was intended to touch everyone. With the exception of the original themes included in this book which have been specifically composed as representative of certain characters and situations, it is wise to bear in mind that better known songs are invariably more effective than those which are less familiar. Our research over the years has provided us with numerous songs with marvelously tempting titles and lyrics. Our experience, however, has taught us that music, in order to work in melodrama, should be immediately recognizeable as serving the purpose for which it is intended. In other words, in melodrama, familiarity breeds content!

A.3) The Piano Player

As we've mentioned, the production of music in melodrama may be as modest or as elaborate as resources permit.

From our own experience, we are quite aware that a shortage of people-power may be a painful fact of life in academic or community theatre. In the case of a melodrama calling only for incidental music, the piano player will act as music director, therefore responsible for the choice of music as well as its execution. As has also been discussed previously, in the production of a musical melodrama the demands upon music director and piano player are likely to be too extensive to be met by one person.

Whatever the duties of the piano player, this individual must definitely be considered one of melodrama's unsung heros or heroines. Consider that rehearsal time is longer than that required of an actor or actress; musical "lines," whether memorized or read, are most likely more numerous than those of any principal. When we add to this the fact that the piano player will probably perform from before the opening curtain to after the final one, we may look upon the piano player as one of the leading roles!

For the piano player or any other musician playing in the semi-darkness of a performance, script and music cues must be easy to follow.

We still recall, with empathetic discomfort, the plight of the piano player who lost his place and had to spend the next several pages of the script frantically rifling through his music in an attempt to catch up. He never really did, and the action onstage was noticeably affected. Fortuntely, this problem arose during a final rehearsal and could be looked on as a lesson well learned rather than the obvious slipup it would have manifested in an actual performance.

Although concentration, complete and constant, is a critical factor in the accompaniment of melodrama, organization is of equal importance. As integral as music is to this classic style, music cues should be scrupulously prepared in order to be easily followed. There are a number of ways to accomplish this task. While we believe that the choice should be made by the piano player or whoever must take the cues, we would stress that it should not be taken lightly.

A.4) The Music Book

Our personal preference is the preparation of a music book similar to the book kept by many directors. Included here is a page from the notebook used during a recent production of *Little Orphan Angela*. Such a book may be made up from plain eight-and-a-half inch by eleven inch notebook paper cut out to frame the disassembled pages of the script. Budget permitting, a much easier approach is to purchase an extra copy of the script and paste its pages back-to-back and centered on either side of the notebook paper.

The notebook paper provides space to enter the cues and fits neatly into a three-ring hardcover looseleaf binder. The standard binder will accept most sheet music and manuscript paper, telescoped if necessary, while its hard cover keeps pages upright and easy to turn. This arrangement enables a musician to integrate all music, incidental or otherwise, directly into the script.

As in the preparation of a garden, the fruits of such effort are readily recognizeable. The alternative can be chaos!

Page 40   *Act I*

PIANO. "Stout-Hearted Men"

ANDY. Yeah, I know. (Snatching his hat off.) I mean, good
evenin', Miss. I met Mr. Tilford as I was ridin' in. He said he was
goin' on ahead to speak to that magic man. Didn't say what for. Said
I was to take you to the social in the buckboard.
RUTH. Land sakes! Here it is pret' near time to go and I'm standin'
here cluckin' like an old hen. You young folks excuse me and I'll
go put myself together. Maybe you can give Angela a hand with the   I LOVE YOU TRULY
basket, Mr. Hanson. I'll only be a minute. (She exits L.) Piano.
ANDY (after an embarrassed pause). Miss, can I help you with the basket?
ANGELA. Oh, no thank you. (Picks up the basket to display it.)
It's all finished.
ANDY. It sure looks pretty, Miss.
ANGELA. Thank you, sir!
ANDY. Well, I . . . (There is another embarrassed silence as they
gaze at one another.) Miss Tilford, I . . . (At the same time,
ANGELA speaks.)

VIOLIN under "Romeo + Juliet"

ANGELA. Mr. Hanson, won't you . . . (They stop, laugh, and gaze
at each other again.)

MOVE L

ANDY (aside). How beautiful she is! She sets me on fire! Could
such an angel ever look with favor on a lowly lumberjack? (To
ANGELA.) I would be right honored if you would call me by my
given name — Andy.

ANGELA (aside). My heart's atwitter! How handsome! *MOVE R*

Continue and segue to Piano "I Think I Love You."

B. The Melo(s) in Melodrama

*(An Alphabetical Listing of Over Three Hundred Musical Selections
Appropriate to the Victorian Era — and How To Use Them)*

There follows an alphabetized listing of songs and themes dating to or prior
to the period during which melodrama enjoyed its prime. This selection of
musical suggestions is by no means complete as there are countless more pieces
appropriate to the period.

Music is listed by title with some subtitles included and categorized by an
additional listing of circumstances.

Many of the selections included here lend themselves to use as certain
themes and are so indicated. We have attempted to provide as many specific
categories as space would permit. Had there been room for such headings as
tired/retired, dances/parades, or *get-lost,* such titles as *The Old Gray Mare,
She Might Have Seen Better Days, The Blue Danube* and even *Shoo Fly, Don't
Bother Me* might have been more suitably identified!

It is hoped, with a touch of imagination on the part of the reader, that the
following will provide music to accompany almost any situation. For example,
look for *celebration* under *triumph* or *demon rum* and consider that some
shady ladies may be *merry widows* and that *departure* is not only *death* but
farewell.

It is suggested by the authors that a healthy helping of humor can go a long
way to contribute to the entertainment. Night and morning music can, for
instance, be applied to unconsciousness or the regaining thereof.

In reference to locations or nationalities, we have taken some liberties with
anachronism. Certain foreign songs which may not date back to the Gay
Nineties per se are sometimes more effective than less familiar ones. When in

66

doubt, a national anthem is often the safest choice and a state college or university song is usually theatrically appropriate if not always historically accurate.

As in describing locations, we believe a certain amount of judicious poetic license to be permissible when choosing themes which mention names. A well-known song with the right name, give or take a few years into the nineteen hundreds, should not be overlooked.

Also indicated are a number of lesser-known songs which are particularly appropriate as olio acts, although creative staging can turn almost any period piece into an effective olio number. Many of these songs may also be adapted to melodramatic scripts which have no music.

Those songs suggested as pre-show warm-up music and for audience sing-alongs represent only a small portion of a choice much too extensive to list herein. It is important that these selections always be recognizable.

Music for most of these songs and many more should be found in the list of reference volumes in the Appendix and in numerous other music books available through public or college libraries.

MANDY LOU at the Southern Appalachian Repertory Theatre

67

THE MELO(S) IN MELODRAMA
Composers and Sources

	sing-along pre-show/M.C.	villain/hero/heroine	comic/pompous/authority	national/patriotic occupations	names/places	home/family/juvenile lullabyes/memories	romance/hope/joy	victory/triumph fight/chase/rescue	stress/fear/trouble disaster/loss/pathos death/departure	shady ladies/dapper dans/demon rum	time/season	land/sea/air	olio
ABSENCE MAKES THE HEART GROW FONDER Arthur Gillespie/Herbert Dillea									X				
AFTER THE BALL Charles K. Harris	X												
AFTER THE DARKNESS													
AH, SWEET MYSTERY OF LIFE Rida Young/Victor Herbert							X						
A-HUNTING WE WILL GO Traditional								X					
AIR FORCE SONG, THE				X								X	
ALEXANDER					X								
ALL HAIL, ARIZONA University of Arizona					X								
ALLOUETTE French Canadian Folk Song					X								
ALL THROUGH THE NIGHT David Owen											X		
ALOHA OE! (Hawaiian Farewell) H. M. Queen Liliuokalani					X				X				
AMERICA, THE BEAUTIFUL Katherine Lee Bates/Samuel A. Ward				X									
ANCHORS AWEIGH Alfred H. Miles/Chas. A. Zimmerman				X								X	
AND HER GOLDEN HAIR WAS HANGING DOWN HER BACK Felix McGlennon/Monroe H. Rosenfeld													X
ANNIE LAURIE (Scottish) Lady John Scott					X								
ANVIL CHORUS, THE ("Il Trovatore") G. Verdi				X				X					
ARKANSAS TRAVELLER American Folk Tune					X								
ARMCHAIR, THE Traditional													X

THE MELO(S) IN MELODRAMA
Composers and Sources

	pre-show/M.C.	sing-along	villain/hero/heroine	comic/pompous/authority	occupations	national/patriotic	names/places	home/family/juvenile	lullabyes/memories	romance/hope/joy	fight/chase/rescue	victory/triumph	stress/fear/trouble	disaster/loss/pathos	death/departure	dans/demon rum	shady ladies/dapper	time/season	land/sea/air	olio
AULD LANG SYNE (Scottish) — Robert Burns									X					X						
BAA! BAA! BLACK SHEEP — Traditional																	X			
BAND PLAYED ON, THE — J. F. Palmer/ C. B. Ward	X																			
BARCAROLLE — Offenbach										X										
BATTLE HYMN OF THE REPUBLIC, THE — Julia Ward Howe/ T. B. Bishop						X														
BEAUTIFUL BROWN EYES — Traditional																				
BEAUTIFUL DREAMER — Stephen Foster									X					X	X					
BEAUTIFUL OHIO — Ballard MacDonald/Mary Earl							X													
BECAUSE — Edward Teschemacher/Guy D'Hardelot										X										
BECAUSE I'M MARRIED NOW																				X
BEETHOVEN'S FIFTH SYMPHONY — Ludwig van Beethoven													X							
BIG ROCK CANDY MOUNTAINS, THE — Greenway/Clark																				X
BILL BAILEY, WON'T YOU PLEASE COME HOME? — Hughie Cannon	X																			
BILLY BOY — American Folk Song							X													
BIRD IN A GILDED CAGE, A — Harry VanTilzer	X													X						
BIRD ON NELLIE'S HAT, THE																				X
BLUE BELL — Morse																				
BLUE BELLS OF SCOTLAND — Scottish Air																				

THE MELO(S) IN MELODRAMA
Composers and Sources

	sing-along pre-show/M.C.	comic/pompous/authority villain/hero/heroine	occupations	names/places national/patriotic	home/family/juvenile	lullabyes/memories	romance/hope/joy	fight/chase/rescue	victory/triumph	stress/fear/trouble	disaster/loss/pathos	death/departure	shady ladies/dapper dans/demon rum	time/season	land/sea/air	olio
BLUE DANUBE WALTZ — Johann Strauss				X												
BOLERO (Spanish) — Ravel				X			X									
BOWERY, THE — Hoyt/Gaunt	X			• X									X			
BREAK THE NEWS TO MOTHER — Charles K. Harris					X											X
BRIDAL CHORUS ("Lohengrin") — Wagner							X									
BUFFALO SKINNERS, THE — Traditional																X
BY THE SEA — Harold R. Atteridge/Harry Carroll	X														X	
CALIFORNIA, HERE I COME — Jolson/DeSylva/Meyer	X			X												
CAN-CAN — Offenbach																X
CAROLINA IN THE MORNING — Kahn/Donaldson	X			X												
CARRY ME BACK TO OLD VIRGINNY — James A. Bland	X			X												
CHEYENNE — Harry Williams/Egbert VanAlstyne																X
CHICAGO	X			X												
CHINATOWN, MY CHINATOWN (Chinese) — Jerome/Schwartz	X			X												
CIRIBIRIBIN — A. Pestalozza		X														X
CLOWN, THE		X														
COME, JOSEPHINE, IN MY FLYING MACHINE — Alfred Bryan/Fred Fisher	X														X	
COME, TAKE A TRIP IN MY AIR SHIP															X	

THE MELO(S) IN MELODRAMA
Composers and Sources

	pre-show/M.C.	sing-along	villain/hero/heroine	comic/pompous/authority	occupations	national/patriotic	names/places	home/family/juvenile	lullabyes/memories	romance/hope/joy	fight/chase/rescue	victory/triumph	stress/fear/trouble	disaster/loss/pathos	death/departure	shady ladies/dapper dans/demon rum	time/season	land/sea/air	olio
COMIN' THROUGH THE RYE — Scottish Air							X												
COMRADES — Felix McGlennon				X															X
COUNTRY GARDENS (Handkerchief Dance) — Traditional							X												
COUSIN JEDEDIAH — H. S. Thompson							X												X
COWBOY'S LIFE IS A DREARY, DREARY LIFE, A — Traditional																			X
CRADLE SONG — Johannes Brahms									X					X			X		
CRIMSON STAIN ("The Ticket-of-Leave Man")																			
CUCKOO, THE — Traditional				X															
CURFEW MUST NOT RING TONIGHT (NELL)																			X
CURSE OF A DREAMER, THE																			
CUSTER'S LAST CHARGE — Traditional																			X
DAISY BELL (BICYCLE BUILT FOR TWO) — Harry Dacre	X															X			
DAKOTA LAND							X												
DANNY BOY — Traditional							X												
DARK EYES — Russian Folk Song							X												
DAY BY DAY																	X		
DEAR OLD DAD (I WANT A GIRL)	X																		
DICKORY, DICKORY DOCK — Traditional																	X		

THE MELO(S) IN MELODRAMA
Composers and Sources

	sing-along / pre-show/M.C.	villain/hero/heroine / comic/pompous/authority	occupations / national/patriotic	names/places	home/family/juvenile / lullabyes/memories	romance/hope/joy	victory/triumph / fight/chase/rescue	stress/fear/trouble / disaster/loss/pathos	death/departure	shady ladies/dapper / dans/demon rum	time/season	land/sea/air	olio
DIXIE — Daniel D. Emmett	X			X									
DON'T GO OUT TONIGHT, DEAR FATHER					X								X
DON'T GO TO THE LION'S CAGE TONIGHT — E. Ray Goetz													X
DOWN BY THE OLD MILL STREAM	X			X									
DRINK TO ME ONLY WITH THINE EYES — Old English Air — Lyrics by Ben Johnson										X			
DRINKING SONG ("The Student Prince") — Donnelly/Romberg										X			
ECHOES OF SPRING											X		
ELSIE FROM CHELSEA — Dacre				X									X
ENTERTAINER, THE — Scott Joplin	X												
EVERYBODY WORKS BUT FATHER — Jean Havez					X								X
EYES OF TEXAS, THE — University of Texas Song				X									
FARMER IN THE DELL, THE — Traditional				X									
FATHER, DEAR FATHER, COME HOME WITH ME NOW — Work					X			X					X
FIGHT, ALABAMA — University of Alabama Song				X									
FLOWERS THAT BLOOM IN THE SPRING, THE — Gilbert/Sullivan		X									X		
FRANKIE AND JOHNNIE — New words & music by Bill Hansen													X
FUNERAL MARCH OF A MARIONETTE — Charles Gounod		X							X				
GAUDEAMUS (Graduation Song)							X						

THE MELO(S) IN MELODRAMA
Composers and Sources

	sing-along pre-show/M.C.	villain/hero/heroine	comic/pompous/authority	occupations national/patriotic	names/places	home/family/juvenile lullabyes/memories	romance/hope/joy	fight/chase/rescue victory/triumph	stress/fear/trouble disaster/loss/pathos death/departure	dans/demon rum shady ladies/dapper	time/season	land/sea/air
GENTLEMEN'S GENTLEMAN ("The Two Orphans")												
GLORY, GLORY, COLORADO — University of Colorado Song					X							
GOD REST YE MERRY, GENTLEMEN											X	
GOOD-BYE									X			
GOOD-BYE, ROSE					X							
GOODNIGHT, LADIES — College Song									X			
HAIL! HAIL! THE GANG'S ALL HERE!							X					
HAIL! MINNESOTA — University of Minnesota Song					X							
HAIL, WEST VIRGINIA — University of West Virginia Song					X							
HEARTS AND FLOWERS									X			
HELLO, CENTRAL, GIVE ME HEAVEN — Charles K. Harris												X
HELLO, MY BABY! — Joseph Howard/Ida Emerson	X											X
HE'S A JOLLY GOOD FELLOW	X											
HINKY, DINKY, PARLEZ VOUS (MADEMOISELLE FROM ARMENTIERES) Traditional French	X				X							
HOME ON THE RANGE — Payne/Bishop						X						
HOME, SWEET HOME — Henry R. Bishop						X						
OO-OO! (AIN'T YOU COMING OUT TONIGHT?)												
HOORAY FOR GAMBLING												X

THE MELO(S) IN MELODRAMA
Composers and Sources

	sing-along pre-show/M.C.	comic/pompous/authority villain/hero/heroine	occupations national/patriotic names/places	home/family/juvenile lullabyes/memories	romance/hope/joy	victory/triumph fight/chase/rescue	stress/fear/trouble disaster/loss/pathos death/departure	shady ladies/dapper dans/demon rum	time/season	land/sea/air	olio
HOP, HOP, HOP! Traditional						X					
HOT TIME IN THE OLD TOWN TONIGHT Joe Hayden/Theo Metz	X					X		X			
HOW'D YOU LIKE TO SPOON WITH ME?											X
HUMORESQUE Dvorak		X				X					
I DON'T WANT TO PLAY IN YOUR YARD H. W. Petrie											X
I LOVE YOU THE SAME OLD WAY Bratton											
I LOVE YOU TRULY Carrie Jacobs-Bond					X						
I PROMISED TO PROTECT HER											
IDAHO, MOTHER OF MINE University of Idaho Song			X								
IF JACK WERE ONLY HERE (MOTHER WAS A LADY) Edward B. Marks/Joseph W. Stern											
ILLINOIS Chamberlain/Jones			X								
ILLINOIS LOYALTY (WE'RE LOYAL TO YOU, ILLINOIS)			X								
ILLINOIS, WE LOVE YOU University of Illinois Song			X								
IN AN OLD DUTCH GARDEN			X								
IN MY MERRY OLDSMOBILE Vincent Bryan/Gus Edwards									X		
IN THE BAGGAGE COACH AHEAD											X
IN THE CITY OF SIGHS AND TEARS Andrew B. Sterlin/Kerry Mills											X
IN THE EVENING BY THE MOONLIGHT James A. Bland	X							X			

74

THE MELO(S) IN MELODRAMA
Composers and Sources

	sing-along / pre-show/M.C.	comic/pompous/authority / villain/hero/heroine	names/places / national/patriotic / occupations	lullabyes/memories / home/family/juvenile	romance/hope/joy	victory/triumph / fight/chase/rescue	death/departure / disaster/loss/pathos / stress/fear/trouble	shady ladies/dapper dans / demon rum	time/season	land/sea/air (olio)
IN THE GOOD OLD SUMMERTIME — Ren Shields/George Evans	X	X		X	X				X	
IN THE SHADE OF THE OLD APPLE TREE — Harry H. Williams/Egbert VanAlstyne	X	X		X	X				X	
INDIANA — Ballard MacDonald/James F. Hanley			X	X						
INDIANA, OUR INDIANA			X							
I'VE BEEN WORKING ON THE RAILROAD — Traditional	X		X							
JEANIE WITH THE LIGHT BROWN HAIR — Stephen Foster		X			X					
JINGLE BELLS — Traditional	X			X					X	
JUANITA — Spanish Air		X			X					
JUST TELL THEM THAT YOU SAW ME — Paul Dresser							X			
KANSAS BOYS — Sandburg			X							
KANSAS FOOL, THE — C. S. Whitney			X							
KEEP ON THE SUNNY SIDE — Drislane/Morse	X	X			X					
KENTUCKY BABE — Richard H. Buck/Adam Geibel			X	X	X					
LA CUCARACHA — Mexican Folk Song		X			X	X				
LA DONNA E MOBILE ("Rigoletto") — G. Verdi		X			X					
LA PALOMA (Spanish) — S. Yradier					X					
REVOLUTIONARY TEA (THERE WAS AN OLD LADY) — Traditional			X							
RHINE SONG (German) — Niklas Becker/G. Kunge			X							X

THE MELO(S) IN MELODRAMA
Composers and Sources

	sing-along pre-show/M.C.	comic/pompous/authority villain/hero/heroine	national/patriotic occupations	names/places	home/family/juvenile	lullabyes/memories	romance/hope/joy	victory/triumph fight/chase/rescue	stress/fear/trouble disaster/loss/pathos	death/departure	shady ladies/dapper dans/demon rum	time/season	land/sea/air	olio
RHODA AND HER PAGODA Adrian Ross/Lionel Monckton														X
ROCK OF AGES Thomas Hastings									X					
ROMEO AND JULIET (LOVE THEME) Tschaikowsky							X							
ROSE OF WASHINGTON SQUARE	X													
ROSE WITH A BROKEN STEM, A														
ROW, ROW, ROW YOUR BOAT (Round) E. O. Lyte	X												X	
RULE, BRITANNIA! (English)		X	X											
SAILING, SAILING Godfrey Marks													X	
SAILOR'S HORNPIPE Traditional													X	
SALOON Earnest R. Ball ("Llab")														X
SCHOOL DAYS					X									
SHE IS MORE TO BE PITIED Gray									X					
SHE MAY HAVE SEEN BETTER DAYS James Thornton									X					
SHE WAS HAPPY TILL SHE MET YOU														X
SHE'LL BE COMIN' 'ROUND THE MOUNTAIN Traditional			X										X	
SHENANDOAH ('CROSS THE WIDE MISSOURI)			X											
LAST ROSE OF SUMMER, THE Old Irish Air ("Groves of Blarney")			X						X					
LEARNING McFADDEN TO WALTZ Fassett/Griswold														X

THE MELO(S) IN MELODRAMA
Composers and Sources

Title / Composer	sing-along pre-show/M.C.	villain/hero/heroine	comic/pompous/authority	occupations	national/patriotic	names/places	home/family/juvenile	lullabyes/memories	romance/hope/joy	fight/chase/rescue	victory/triumph	stress/fear/trouble	disaster/loss/pathos	death/departure	dans/demon rum	shady ladies/dapper	time/season	land/sea/air	olio
LET ME CALL YOU SWEETHEART — Beth Slater Whetson/Leo Friedman	X																		
LETTER EDGED IN BLACK — Hattie Nevada Traditional																			X
LIEBESTRAUME THEME (LOVE DREAMS) — Franz Liszt									X										
LIFE IN CALIFORNIA																			X
LISTEN TO THE MOCKING BIRD — Traditional			X																
LITTLE ANNIE ROONEY — Michael Nolan																			X
LITTLE BROWN JUG — Traditional															X				
LITTLE LOST CHILD, THE — Edward B. Marks/Joseph W. Stern																			X
LITTLE TOMMY TINKER (Round) — Traditional	X																		
LONG, LONG AGO — Thomas H. Bayly								X											
LOUSY MINER, THE ("The Spoilers") — John A. Stone																			X
LOVE'S OLD SWEET SONG — G. Clifton Bingham/James L. Malloy								X	X										
MacDONALD'S FARM — Traditional				X															
MAMIE — Will D. Cobb/Gus Edwards				X															
MAN ON THE FLYING TRAPEZE, THE — Traditional	X	X																X	
MAN WHO BROKE THE BANK AT MONTE CARLO, THE — Fred Gilbert															X				X
MANSION OF ACHING HEARTS, THE — Andrew J. Lamb/Harry Von Tilzer																			X
MAPLE LEAF FOREVER, THE (Canadian) — Alexander Muir					X														

THE MELO(S) IN MELODRAMA

Composers and Sources

	pre-show/M.C.	sing-along	villain/hero/heroine	comic/pompous/authority	occupations	national/patriotic	names/places	home/family/juvenile	lullabyes/memories	romance/hope/joy	fight/chase/rescue	victory/triumph	stress/fear/trouble	disaster/loss/pathos	death/departure	dans/demon rum	shady ladies/dapper	time/season	land/sea/air	olio
MAPLE LEAF RAG (Canadian) Scott Joplin							X													
MARCH OF THE TOYS Victor Herbert/John A. Harighton								X												
MARCHE SLAVE THEME Tschaikowsky																				
MARCHING THROUGH GEORGIA							X													
MARIE, AH, MARIE (Italian)							X													
MARSEILLAISE (French National Anthem) J. Rouget De L'Isle							X													
MARY KELLY'S BEAU Edward Harrigan/Dave Braham																				X
MARY'S A GRAND OLD NAME George M. Cohan	X						X													
MEET ME IN ST. LOUIS Andrew B. Sterling/Kerry Mills	X						X													
MEMORIES Gus Kahn/Egbert VanAlstyne								X												
MEN OF PENNSYLVANIA							X													
MERRY WIDOW WALTZ, THE Franz Lehar															X		X			
MICHAEL, ROW THE BOAT ASHORE Jay Arnold							X												X	
MICHIGAN, MY MICHIGAN Malloch/Meissner							X													
MIDNIGHT FIRE ALARM Harry J. Lincoln																				X
MIGHTY OREGON University of Oregon Song							X													
MINUET IN G Ludwig Van Beethoven															X					
MOBILE BAY																				

THE MELO(S) IN MELODRAMA
Composers and Sources

	sing-along pre-show/M.C.	villain/hero/heroine	comic/pompous/authority	occupations	national/patriotic	names/places	home/family/juvenile	lullabyes/memories	romance/hope/joy	fight/chase/rescue	victory/triumph	stress/fear/trouble	disaster/loss/pathos	death/departure	dans/demon rum	shady ladies/dapper	time/season	land/sea/air	olio
MOLLY AND I AND THE BABY						X													
MORNING ("Peer Gynt")																	X		
MOTHER							X												
MOTHER MACREE (Irish)							X												
MOTHER WAS A LADY Edward B. Marks/Joseph W. Stern																			X
MY BONNIE Traditional	X																	X	
MY GAL SAL Paul Dresser	X					X													
MY GRANDFATHER'S CLOCK Henry C. Work																	X		
MY HERO Stanislaus Stange/Docar Straus		X																	
MY OLD KENTUCKY HOME Stephen Foster							X												
MY SWEETHEART'S THE MAN IN THE MOON James Thornton																			X
MY WILD IRISH ROSE Chauncey Olcott							X												
NEARER, MY GOD TO THEE Lowell Mason													X						
NO LETTERS FROM HOME H. C. Work																			X
NO! NO! A THOUSAND TIMES, NO! Al Sherman/Al Lewis/Abner Silver																			
NOBODY Alex Rogers/Bert A. Williams																			X
NONE BUT THE LONELY HEART Tschaikowsky																			
NOW THE DAY IS OVER Baring-Gould/Barnaby																	X		

THE MELO(S) IN MELODRAMA
Composers and Sources

Song / Composer	sing-along pre-show/M.C.	villain/hero/heroine	comic/pompous/authority occupations	national/patriotic names/places	home/family/juvenile	lullabyes/memories	romance/hope/joy	fight/chase/rescue	victory/triumph	stress/fear/trouble	disaster/loss/pathos	death/departure	shady ladies/dapper dans/demon rum	time/season	land/sea/air	olio
O SOLE MIO (Italian) — E. DeCapna				X												
OH, DEM GOLDEN SLIPPERS	X												X			
OH! HOW SO FAIR (MARTHA) — F. von Flotow				X												
OH! I'VE LOST IT!																X
OH, MY DARLING CLEMENTINE — Percy Montrose	X			X										X		
OH, PROMISE ME						X										
OH! SUSANNA — Stephen Foster	X			X												
OH, YOU BEAUTIFUL DOLL — A. Seymour Brown/Nat D. Ayer	X												X			
OKLAHOMA, HAIL — University of Oklahoma Song				X												
OLD GRAY MARE, THE — Traditional	X	X			X											
OLD MISSOURI — University of Missouri Song				X												
OLD OAKEN BUCKET, THE — Katherine Lee Bates/C. Krallmark																
OLD SETTLER'S SONG, THE																X
OLD SHANTY TOWN — Young/Siras	X															
ON A SUNDAY AFTERNOON — Andrew B. Sterling/Harry VonTilzer														X		
ON, IOWA				X												
ON THE BANKS OF THE WABASH — Paul Dresser				X												
ON THE ROAD TO DELAWARE — University of Delaware Song				X												

THE MELO(S) IN MELODRAMA
Composers and Sources

	sing-along pre-show/M.C.	villain/hero/heroine	comic/pompous/authority	occupations national/patriotic	names/places	home/family/juvenile	lullabyes/memories	romance/hope/joy	fight/chase/rescue	victory/triumph	stress/fear/trouble	disaster/loss/pathos	death/departure	dans/demon rum	shady ladies/dapper	time/season	land/sea/air	olio
ON, WISCONSIN — University of Wisconsin Song	X																	
OUR CHICAGO — University of Chicago Song	X																	
OUR GOLDEN WEDDING DAY (OLD GRAY BONNET)	X						X											
PACK OF CARDS — Traditional																		X
PAL OF MINE																		
PARADE OF THE WOODEN SOLDIERS — Albert Gamse/Leon Jessel		X																
PARDON CAME TOO LATE, THE — Paul Dresser																		
PEEK-A-BOO																		
PIANO CONCERTO NO. 1 — Tschaikowsky																		
PICTURE THAT IS TURNED TO THE WALL, THE												X						X
PIG GOT UP AND SLOWLY WALKED AWAY, THE																		X
PLAYMATES — Harry Dacre						X												
PLEASE, FATHER, LET US IN (LILLIE OF THE SNOWSTORM) H. C. Work																		X
POMP AND CIRCUMSTANCE										X								
POP GOES THE WEASEL — Traditional American										X								
QUILTING PARTY, THE (I WAS SEEING NELLIE HOME) Traditional																		X
R-E-M-O-R-S-E — George Ade/Alfred G. Wathall																		X
REUBEN AND RACHEL — Harry Birch/William Gooch																		X

THE MELO(S) IN MELODRAMA
Composers and Sources

	sing-along pre-show/M.C.	villain/hero/heroine	comic/pompous/authority	occupations	national/patriotic	names/places	home/family/juvenile	lullabyes/memories	romance/hope/joy	fight/chase/rescue	victory/triumph	stress/fear/trouble	disaster/loss/pathos	death/departure	dans/demon rum	shady ladies/dapper	time/season	land/sea/air	olio
REVILLE (I HATE TO GET UP IN THE MORNING)																	X		
SHINE ON, HARVEST MOON	X																X		
SHOO FLY, DON'T BOTHER ME																			
SHUBERT'S SERENADE Franz Shubert									X										
SIDEWALKS OF NEW YORK, THE (EAST SIDE, WEST SIDE) Charles B. Lawlor/James W. Blake	X				X														
SILVER HEELS (INTERMEZZO) (American Indian) James O'Dea/Neil Moret					X														
SILVER THREADS AMONG THE GOLD H. P. Danks								X											
SINCE DADDY'S BEEN TAKEN AWAY								X											X
SMILES J. Will Callahan/Lee Roberts	X										X								
SODA AND B— Traditional																			X
SONG OF INDIA, A (Indian) Rimsky-Korsakoff					X														
SONG OF LOVE (SHUBERT'S SERENADE) Shubert									X										
SONG OF THE VOLGA BOATMEN (Russian) Russian Folk Song					X													X	
SONGS MY MOTHER TAUGHT ME Anton Dvorak																			
STARS AND STRIPES FOREVER John P. Souza			X		X						X								
STARS OF THE SUMMER NIGHT Longfellow/Woodbury																	X		
STEIN SONG University of Maine Song					X														
STOUTHEARTED MEN Hammerstein/Romberg		X																	

82

THE MELO(S) IN MELODRAMA
Composers and Sources

	sing-along / pre-show/M.C.	comic/pompous/authority / villain/hero/heroine	occupations / national/patriotic	names/places / home/family/juvenile	lullabyes/memories	romance/hope/joy	victory/triumph / fight/chase/rescue	stress/fear/trouble / disaster/loss/pathos	death/departure	shady ladies/dapper dans / demon rum	time/season	land/sea/air
STRIKE UP THE BAND (HERE COMES A SAILOR) Andrew B. Sterling/Charles B. Ward												
SURPRISE SYMPHONY Haydn							X					
SUSY, LITTLE SUSY Traditional				X								
SWEET ADELINE Richard H. Girard/Harry Armstrong	X			X								
SWEET AND LOW Joseph Barnby				X								X
SWEET GENEVIEVE				X								
SWEET MARIE C. Warman/Raymond Moore				X								
SWEET ROSIE O'GRADY (Irish) Maude Nugent	X			X								
SWEETEST STORY EVER TOLD, THE R. M. Stultz					X							
TA-RA-RA-BOOM DER-E Henry J. Sayers	X						X			X		
TALE OF A BUMBLEBEE, THE Frank Pixley/Gustav Luders												X
TALES FROM THE VIENNA WOODS WALTZ Johann Strauss				X								
TAPS									X		X	
THERE IS A TAVERN IN THE TOWN Traditional Old Cornish Air	X									X		
THERE'S A LONG, LONG TRAIL A-WINDING					X	X						
THERE'S NOTHING WE CAN SAY BUT JUST GOODBYE												
THINE ALONE					X							
THREE BLIND MICE (Round) Traditional	X	X										

THE MELO(S) IN MELODRAMA
Composers and Sources

Title / Composers and Sources	sing-along pre-show/M.C.	villain/hero/heroine	comic/pompous/authority	national/patriotic occupations	names/places	home/family/juvenile	lullabyes/memories	romance/hope/joy	fight/chase/rescue	victory/triumph	stress/fear/trouble	disaster/loss/pathos	death/departure	dans/demon rum	shady ladies/dapper	time/season	land/sea/air	olio
TILL THE SANDS OF THE DESERT GROW COLD George Graff/Ernest Ball																		
TILL WE MEET AGAIN Egan/Whiting													X					
TIPTOE THROUGH THE TULIPS WITH ME (Dutch) Al Dubin/Joe Benke					X													
TIT-WILLOW ("Mikado") Gilbert/Sullivan			X													X		
TOREADOR THEME ("Carmen") (Spanish) Bizet										X								
TOYLAND Glen MacDonough/Victor Herbert						X												
TURKEY IN THE STRAW American Folk Theme			X		X													
TRIUMPHAL MARCH ("Aida") G. Verdi										X								
TWINKLE, TWINKLE, LITTLE STAR Jane Taylor																X		
TWO GUITARS Russian Gypsy Song					X													
UNCLE SAM'S FARM Jesse Hutchinson, Jr.																		X
UNDER THE ANHEUSER BUSH Andrew B. Sterling/Harry Von Tilzer																		X
UNDERNEATH THE ARCHES																		
UPPER TEN AND THE LOWER FIVE, THE sung by Lawlor/Thornton																		X
UTAH MAN University of Utah Song					X													
VACANT CHAIR, THE Washburn/Root												X						
VERMONT VICTORIOUS University of Vermont Song					X													
WAIT FOR THE WAGON Traditional					X													

THE MELO(S) IN MELODRAMA
Composers and Sources

	sing-along pre-show/M.C.	villain/hero/heroine	comic/pompous/authority	national/patriotic occupations	names/places	home/family/juvenile	lullabyes/memories	romance/hope/joy	victory/triumph fight/chase/rescue	stress/fear/trouble disaster/loss/pathos	death/departure	dans/demon rum	shady ladies/dapper	time/season	land/sea/air	olio
WAIT TILL THE CLOUDS ROLL BY (JENNY)					X											
WAIT TILL THE SUN SHINES, NELLIE Vincent Bryan/Gus Edwards	X				X											
WAITING AT THE CHURCH Fred W. Leigh/Henry E. Pether																X
WALTZ ME AROUND AGAIN, WILLIE Will D. Cobb/Ren Shields																X
WASTE NOT, WANT NOT																X
WATCHING FOR PA H. C. Work																
WE SAIL THE OCEAN BLUE ("H. M.S. Pinafore") Gilbert/Sullivan															X	
WEARING OF THE GREEN (Irish) Traditional					X											
WHEN GRANDMAMA IS GONE																
WHEN IRISH EYES ARE SMILING Olcott/Graff/Ball	X				X											
WHEN MOTHER FELL ASLEEP																
WHEN YOU WERE SWEET SIXTEEN James Thornton						X										
WHEN YOU WORE A TULIP	X															
WHERE IS MY WANDERING BOY TONIGHT? Reverend R. Lowry																X
WHO IS SYLVIA? Franz Schubert					X											
WHO THREW THE OVERALLS IN MISTRESS MURPHY'S CHOWDER? George L. Giefer																X
WILL YOU LOVE ME IN DECEMBER? Ernest R. Ball/James Walker																
WILLIAM TELL OVERTURE Rossini									X							

THE MELO(S) IN MELODRAMA
Composers and Sources
(including Addendum)

	sing-along pre-show/M.C.	villain/hero/heroine	comic/pompous/authority occupations	national/patriotic names/places	home/family/juvenile	lullabyes/memories	romance/hope/joy	fight/chase/rescue	victory/triumph	stress/fear/trouble	disaster/loss/pathos	death/departure	dans/demon rum	shady ladies/dapper	time/season	land/sea/air	olio
WITH ALL HER FAULTS, I LOVE HER STILL / Rosenfeld																	
WOODMAN, SPARE THAT TREE / Morris/Russell																	X
WORK, FOR THE NIGHT IS COMING / Walker-Coghill/Mason															X		
YANKEE DOODLE / Traditional	X			X													
YELLOW ROSE OF TEXAS / Traditional, adapted by Chester Nordman				X													
YOU TELL ME YOUR DREAM / Charles Daniels	X																
YOU'RE NOT THE ONLY PEBBLE ON THE BEACH Harry Braisted/Stanley Carter																	X
COLOMBIA, THE GEM OF THE OCEAN / Traditional, with text by Thomas a Becket				X					X								
DEUTSCHLAND UBER ALLES / German National Anthem				X													
HAIL TO THE CHIEF / Sir Walter Scott/James Sanderson			X														
SALLY IN OUR ALLEY / Carey/Beethoven				X													

86

VICTORY

Doom (VICTORY FOR VILLAIN)

FINE

EARLY-MORNING THEM

("BIRDIES")

(Repeat as Necessary)

In "2"

Sostenuto

(AFTER LAST TIME)

FINE

Chase - "To The Rescue"

Chase/Fight

Repeat as necessary

LOVE THEME

COMIC

HEROINE'S THEME

VILLAIN'S THEME

DISASTER

TROUBLE'S COMING

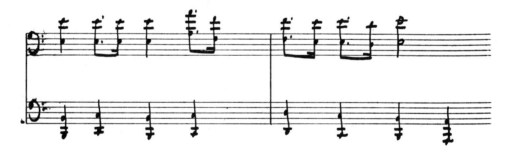

HERO'S THEME

(MARCH)

100

LULLABY

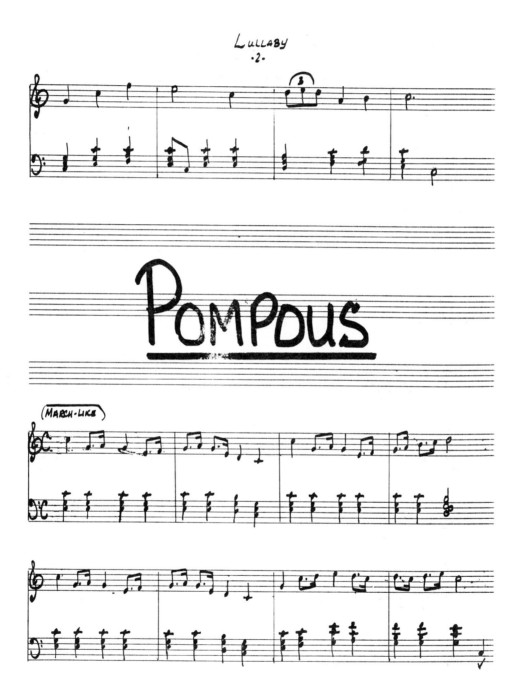

PATHOS

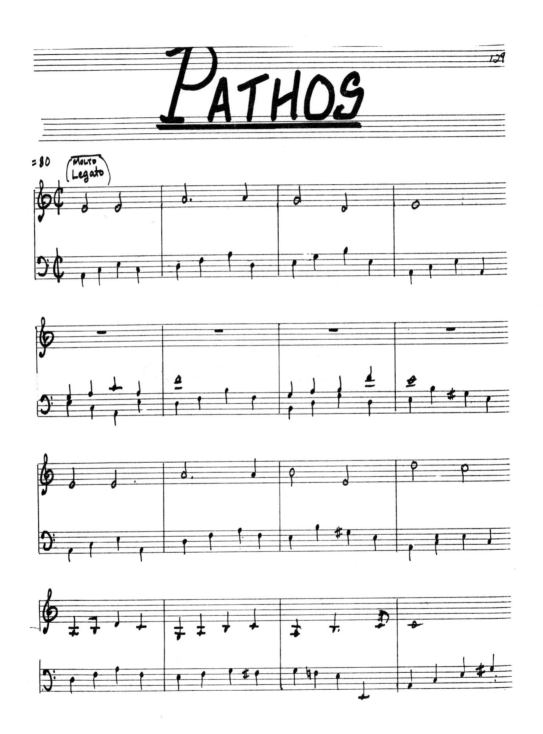

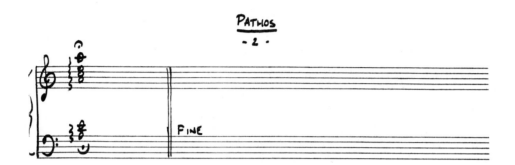

4th of July Frolic

a high flying musical

MELODRAMA

DASTARDLY DEEDS AT A 170 FLY IN

Saluting the International Cessna 170 Association

The whole family can join in the fun... CHEER, BOO, HISS, SIP (beverages) MUNCH (popcorn) and SING-ALONG!

July 4th – 8:00pm
Fresno Hilton Hotel (ballroom)
Admission $5⁰⁰

Tickets available from:
Bob Anderson 233-8983
Ralph Gazarian 834-2194
John Pugliese 229-5273
also at the door

Starring members of:
Golden Chain Theatre - Oakhurst
Squirrel Cage Theatre - Northfork
Grub Gulch Garter Girls, Guys & Grannies

in a cliff-hanging saga of lecherous pilots, helpless maidens, perilous predicaments, hairbreadth rescues...and to break the suspense some hilarious olio-acts.

106

CHAPTER IV

Selling Melodrama

Good publicity is critical to the ultimate success of any theatrical endeavor. Melodrama should be publicized and sold like any other theatrical product. This calls for lots of advance planning and organization on the part of a publicity manager who is capable and dependable and has an outgoing personality.

Academic theatre is always funded — to some degree at least — and the goal of most community theatre is to break even (at least!). Therefore, sales are important. If your production is intended to be a fund-raiser, sales are even more important. There's not a product in existence which cannot be sold to the right buyer when properly marketed. No matter how good your show may be, you won't have a show at all unless you have an audience. Step one is to insure a good audience and the best way to do this is through good publicity.

A. Posters

Posters such the one on page 106 may be printed on brightly-colored paper and placed in the windows of local stores and everywhere else they are allowed. Obviously, a well-designed, well-executed poster suggests a well-planned production. If the budget prohibits a professional printing job, you had best enlist your top artist along with a friend who has access to a copy machine. As in all advertising, repetition is most effective. A single identifiable logo will be more noticeable and more memorable than an inconsistent variety of designs.

B. The Media

Radio, television, newspapers and many other publications are good sources of publicity. For the non-profit organization, all of these are likely to be free.

Radio stations are required by law to donate time to public service announcements (psa's). Properly prepared copy is important and should be submitted two to three weeks in advance. We like to use colored paper for such

GOLDEN CHAIN THEATRE

P.O. BOX 604   OAKHURST, CALIF. 93644

KMJ-TV 24   June 1, 1978
1544 Van Ness Ave.
Fresno, California 99728

Attention: Dick Moody

Dear Dick,

    As you will see by the enclosed material, it's
melodrama time again,
    We of the Golden Chain Theatre are grateful for
the support KMJ-TV has given us in the past and will
appreciate any (and every!) mention you and your staff
may be able to give us this 1978 season.
    As always we look forward to seeing you at one of
our productions and, of course, hope you will drop in
with your camera man sometime previous to our opening.

Cordially,

Joan L. Bushnell
Manager, Public Relations

GOLDEN CHAIN THEATRE

Box E. Bass Lake,
California 93604

(209)877-2755

GOLDEN CHAIN THEATRE

P.O. BOX 604   OAKHURST, CALIF. 93644

Attention: Public Service   July 10, 1978

Gentlemen:

We will appreciate your including the following information
in your public service or coming events announcements during
the week of July 31st:

THE GOLDEN CHAIN THEATRE, OAKHURST, PROUDLY ANNOUNCES THE

WORLD PREMIERE OF ITS NEWEST MUSICAL MELODRAMA, "MISS MELODY'S

LAMENT, OR DIRTY DEEDS ON DECK!" THURSDAY, AUGUST 3RD.

PERFORMANCES, INCLUDING OLIO ACTS, AUDIENCE SING-ALONGS, AND

THE FABULOUS DANCING OF THE DAZZLING GRUB GULCH GARTER GIRLS

AND GRANNIES, RUN FRIDAY AND SATURDAY EVENINGS THROUGH

SEPTEMBER 9TH. CURTAIN TIME IS 8:15. THERE WILL BE ONE SUNDAY

MATINEE AUGUST 27TH AT 2:30. CABARET SEATING, WITH BEER, SOFT

DRINKS, POP CORN AND HOT DOGS AVAILABLE, IS FOUR DOLLARS PER

PERSON. FOR RESERVATIONS, CALL THE GOLDEN CHAIN THEATRE,

683-7112, WEEKDAYS BETWEEN 1:00 AND 6:00 P.M.. CALL 683-7112

FOR AN EVENING OF FAMILY FUN AT THE GOLDEN CHAIN THEATRE,

JUST TWO MILES NORTH OF OAKHURST ON HIGHWAY 41.

Joan L. Bushnell
Manager, Public Relations

GOLDEN CHAIN THEATRE

(209) 877-2755

HELLO, THERE, (CALL LETTERS, TOWN) THIS IS JOANIE BUSHNELL FOR THE GOLDEN CHAIN THEATRE, OAKHURST! WE'RE HERE TO TELL YOU THAT THE GOLDEN CHAIN THEATRE, ON HIGHWAY 41 TWO MILES NORTH OF OAKHURST, ANNOUNCES THE OPENING OF A BRAND NEW MELODRAMA, "THE CURSE OF THE ACHING HEART, OR TRAPPED IN THE SPIDER'S WEB," THURSDAY, AUGUST 7TH. CURTAIN TIME IS AT 8:15 P.M. PERFORMANCES RUN FRIDAY AND SATURDAY EVENINGS THROUGH SEPTEMBER 13TH. CABARET SEATING, WITH BEER, SOFT DRINKS, AND POPCORN AVAILABLE, IS THREE-FIFTY PER PERSON. FOR RESERVATIONS CALL THE GOLDEN CHAIN THEATRE, 683–7112. CALL 683–7112 FOR AN EVENING OF FAMILY FUN AT THE GOLDEN CHAIN THEATRE.

(Thanks to the help of a friend employed by a local studio, this copy was taped over music. Tapes were then mailed to every radio station within a three-hour drive of the theatre. The results were excellent!)

June 8, 1979

Gentlemen:

We will appreciate your including the following information in your Public Service or Coming Events Announcements during the week of June 25th:

"THREE CHEERS FOR THE YONDER, WILD AND BLUE!" . . . THE INTERNATIONAL CESSNA ONE-SEVENTY ASSOCIATION WILL PRESENT A MUSICAL MELODRAMA WEDNESDAY EVENING, JULY 4TH IN THE GRAND BALLROOM OF THE FRESNO HILTON HOTEL . . . CURTAIN TIME IS 8:00 P.M. . . . CABARET SEATING, WITH BEVERAGES AND POPCORN AVAILABLE, IS $5.00 PER PERSON . . . TICKETS WILL BE SOLD AT THE DOOR . . . FOR MUSICAL MELODRAMA WITH DANCING GIRLS, SING-ALONG, OLIO ENTERTAINMENT, COME PILOTS, COME CO-PILOTS, COME FLY WITH US AT THE FRESNO HILTON HOTEL, JULY 4TH AT 8:00 P.M.!

"THREE CHEERS FOR THE YONDER, WILD AND BLUE!"

Joan L. Bushnell
(209) 877-2755

releases — anything to catch the eye of the program director!

Many television stations picture a selection of posters with their psa's. Have your publicity manager contact local stations well in advance as posters must be delivered three to four weeks before they are to be aired. If you're lucky, you may be able to coax a television cameraman to one of your final dress rehearsals. Be prepared with a fact sheet giving all the important details regarding your show and you may see some footage of your production on the evening news!

Hopefully, radio and television coverage will run through the week prior to opening and be repeated at regular intervals if the run is a long one.

C. The Press

A proficient writer is a valuable asset to publicizing your production. A well-written and properly-submitted press release may not be printed in its original form, but it is a sure way to catch the attention of any editor. As with the visual impact in a poster, a well-prepared article suggests a well-planned show. The *inverted pyramid* so often used in journalism is the best approach to an article for a newspaper. The inverted pyramid is just what it sounds like — all the heavy information at the top, dwindling down to the extras at the bottom. Such a form makes it possible for an editor to cut the length of the article as necessary with little or no rewriting. Who-what-where-when-why and if there's space, *how* is a good formula to follow in the preparation of your article. The name of your organization or production should be mentioned at least three times for impact. Unless a longer article is specifically requested, it is invariably more effective to fit all of your material onto a single page.

When possible, newspaper coverage should run at least three times prior to your show's opening. To keep your product in people's minds, there are many angles or slants for the same old information, and more than one writer at work tends to turn out fresher material. Try to have a cast list published immediately following auditions. Next, go for a story about rehearsals. Finally, submit an announcement of the big opening!

Most newspapers, particularly the smaller ones, will be delighted to give you coverage if you can provide pictures. That a single picture is worth more than a thousand words is a proven fact in the newspaper business. Although it is the policy of many major newspapers to use their own photographers, a picture may get you the attention of a busy editor where an article without one could get you lost in the shuffle. Here, then, is a job for your prize photographer!

C.1) Publicity Pictures

Publicity pictures should portray scenes from your upcoming production, complete with costume and makeup. If some scenery or setpieces are available, so much the better. The most important aspect, however, is to capture an active shot which will catch the reader's attention. After all, who's going to linger over a lineup of characters standing side by side when there's something more interesting to look at on the next page? The standard required by most publications is the 8" x 10" black and white print with glossy finish. The name of your organization, production, production dates, the names of the people in the picture identified left to right, a credit for the photographer and a telephone number for further information should be noted on the back of each print. A felt-tip pen is easy to read and will not damage the photo.

C.2) The Mail

The use of direct mail is another way to publicize. Although this is an excellent means of reaching a large number of people and taking advance reservations, printing and mailing costs (even at the bulk rate) can be considerable. Also, there is a need for a mailing list and people to address. Because of all this, we would only recommend the use of direct mail if your show is scheduled for a long run or if your group produces regularly.

As an inexpensive alternative to direct mail, we have used "hand-outs" to publicize short-running productions. To make a master copy for hand-outs, divide a sheet of 8 1/2" x 11" typing paper into six parts, then type your information into each section. Be sure these hand-outs are designed so as not to be confused with tickets. With access to a copier, a hundred or more sheets of copy paper, and a pair of scissors, you will quite quickly have six hundred or more hand-outs to distribute at student or community functions, to local businesses, or to place as stuffers in other mailings. The new, brightly-colored Astro Paper available in some copy stores is excellent for this purpose.

Newsletters are often a good source of publicity. If any members of your group are involved in organizations which issue periodical newsletters, be sure to ask if your show may be mentioned.

All publicity within the bounds of good taste is good publicity. Any contact with radio, television, newspapers or anyone else who can let the public know about your show may mean another filled seat when the curtain rises. And this is what makes it all worth all the work on *everyone's* part!

CHAPTER V

Frills, Fun and Frolic

Hamlet said, "The play's the thing!"

With all due respect to the tragic Dane, the play's not the only thing in the presentation of successful melodrama. In fact, it's just the beginning! As a nineteenth-century form, this classic style affords an opportunity to peek into the past which should not be passed up. In order to be fully enjoyed today, melodrama should be presented not just as a play, but as a production.

Like the frosting and the trimmings on a cake, there are lots of frills with which to "decorate" melodrama and turn that play into fun and frolic for all involved. In this respect, the energies of the director must be broad in scope. The objective is to coordinate the play itself with music, stage effect, variety entertainment, general atmosphere — all the elements needed to present the melodramatic play as a total theatrical experience.

Nineteenth-century melodrama thrived because it was the drama of the people. Twentieth-century melodrama should be much the same inasmuch as it is dependent for its success upon the response of the people, or audience reaction and participation. In order to encourage audience participation, it's important to establish an atmosphere as early as possible.

There are numerous theatre groups which specialize in melodrama, some few of which are listed at the end of this section. If you should have access to a theatre patterned on the Gay Nineties, lucky you! If not, melodrama, more than most theatre forms, lends itself to a wide variety of conditions. Historical accuracy is a prerequisite, of course. Theatrical appropriateness may be achieved in a variety of ways.

A. The Greeter

There's no better place to begin your show than at the door where a "greeter" may be stationed to welcome the audience upon arrival. The greeter might say, for instance, "Welcome to East Lynne!" (or whatever other title befits). The greeter may also hand out programs patterned on the old-fashioned long and narrow style with lyrics for audience sing-alongs printed on the back.

B. The Programs

The original melodrama programs, printed on pink newspaper, were known as "pink sheets." If possible, pink sheets add to the atmosphere; if not, regular newspaper is more effective and less expensive than heavier paper.

The greeter also directs those who need to purchase tickets or pay admission to the box office. In some melodrama groups, the greeter is also the master or mistress of ceremonies, but more about this later.

C. The Box Office

The box office, like many other aspects of your production, may be as sophisticated or as simple as conditions allow. Tickets may be run off on a copy machine in the pattern of the handouts as described in the section on publicity or, if you can arrange for it, they may be printed by some local business whose name will appear on the back. If your show is scheduled for a long run and you have the funds, you may order computer printed tickets from one of the national companies specializing in this process. The advantage here is that tickets are color-coded and dated for each performance and may be numbered by tables and seats.

If you prefer not to use tickets at all, admission may be taken at the door. This approach, although less complicated in some ways, precludes any advance sale of seats as well as an accurate attendance count. For smaller productions or those with a short run, a long table with space for cash box(es) and all other necessary material may be covered in red, purple, pink or gold — popular colors generally associated with the period. Box office personnel, like all others seen by the audience, should be in costume.

It's always fun, when possible, to decorate the lobby or entry with pictures of the cast in makeup and costume and/or captioned scenes from the production. This display is easily accomplished with large posterboard and easels. Proving once again that there's something for everyone in theatre, here's a job for your photographer and artist!

GOLDEN CHAIN THEATRE

2 Miles North of Oakhurst, CA   Phone 683-7112

commemorates its tenth anniversary

with the

WORLD PREMIERE PERFORMANCE

of

LITTLE ORPHAN ANGELA

or

"The Magician's Dirty Tricks!"

by

Charles H. Randall and Joan L. Bushnell
Music and Lyrics by Joan L. Bushnell

PERFORMANCES FRIDAY AND SATURDAY EVENINGS THROUGH JULY 30, 1977

The dramatic action transpires in and around Fresno Flats, a community which later changed its name to Oakhurst. The spectacular scenic effects were designed by that Captain of Craftsmanship, the indefatigable **MR. J. FRANK MARTIN.** The complex chores of construction rested chiefly in the capable hands of **MR. SARGE SARGENTINI.** The astounding scene painting is ample evidence of the amazing artistry of **MRS. CAROL SAVAGE** and **MRS. JANE GYER.**

IMPORTANT! If you expect to rate as a gentleman, do not expectorate on the floor!

MR. CHARLES H. RANDALL'S directorial diligence has been dedicated to designing the dazzling demonstration of dramatic deportment displayed with deft distinction by the devoted disciples of drama. This debilitating deed was definitely decreased by delegating diverse duties to his delightful and dedicated deputies, **MRS. CRYSTAL ANDREWS** and **MRS. MURIEL CARLSON.**

MRS. JOAN L. BUSHNELL, as musical director mischievously managed the melodious melodies, with the indispensable aid of **MR. CHESTER HAYDEN** as vocal coach.

HISSING, BOOING AND CHEERING ARE ENCOURAGED! ALL SCREAMS, HOWEVER, WILL BE INVESTIGATED!

The titilating tunes and merry melodies are the product of the dazzling digital dexterity of those unparalleled artists of the ivories, **MRS. JACKIE BYERS** or **MISS LOLA M. RICHMOND.**

FEATURING THE FOLLOWING STELLAR CAST

MR. LES WILLIAMS as Solomon Tilford, a tireless and truly trustworthy toiler, touched by tragedy by a tyrant's treachery.

MRS. NORMA LUNZ as Ruth Tilford, Solomon's soul-mate and staunch supporter, somewhat susceptable to sorrow.

MRS. JAYNITA CRAIN as Angela Tilford, an appropriately appreciated adopted angel acutely attracted to amiable Andy.

MR. JEFF SAVAGE as Andy Hanson, a husky handsome humble hero who has high hopes of happiness.

MR. RICHARD WARNOCK as Sheriff Marshall, a modest, mild-mannered magistrate who meets and masters a malicious miscreant.

MR. GLEN WALSH as Ned Penny, a provincial proletarian, possessed of the personality of a playful puppy.

MR. RUSSELL SHORT as Ignatius B. Cutworthy, a crafty contemptible cad whose coldly calculated connivance creates considerable consternation.

MRS. LA RETTA ROOPE as Imogene Cutworthy, cruelly cast as Cutworthy's conscience-stricken co-conspirator.

MR. GEORGE BUSHNELL, MISS BETH CLEMENTS, MRS. JULIE EATON, MRS. LIZ GORSKI, MR. JACK GYER, MR. PAUL KEEL, MISS GWEN LOPEZ, MR. JERRY ROOPE, MR. GUY ROSE, and MRS. MARGARET SADLER as robust rural residents redolent with radiant rusticity.

MRS. CANDY EARNEST, MRS. VICKI ELLIOTT, MRS. PAT KELLOGG, MRS. DE LOIS ROSE, MRS. MARCIA WILKINS as Cutworthy's Cuties, a covey of captivating, curvaceous chorines whose kicks and capers contribute to Cutworthy's carnival caravan.

SYNOPSIS

MISTRESS OF CEREMONIES . . . . . . MRS. MURIEL CARLSON
CAN CAN danced by the **GRUB GULCH GARTER GIRLS**
ACT ONE Scene 1: Fresno Flats
OLIO: We'll Always Be Sweethearts sung by **MR. JERRY ROOPE**
Be My Little Bumble Bee danced by the **GRUB GULCH CARTER GIRLS**
ACT ONE Scene 2: The Tilford's Farm Kitchen
OLIO: An Irish Medley sung by **MRS. LA RETTA ROOPE**
and **MR. JERRY ROOPE**
In The Good Ol' Summer Time danced by the
GRUB GULCH GRANNIES and GRANDADS
ACT ONE Scene 3: In Grub Gulch
★ ★ ★ ★ **INTERMISSION** ★ ★ ★ ★
OLIO: The Bagpipes of **MR. WILLIAM DICK**
ACT TWO Scene 1: In Grub Gulch
OLIO: Alice Blue Gown sung by **MRS. MURIEL CARLSON**
OLIO: I Don't Care sung by **MRS. VICKI ELLIOTT** and **MRS. LIZ GORSKI**
ACT TWO Scene 2: The Tilford Kitchen
OLIO: China Town danced by the **GRUB GULCH GARTER GIRLS**
ACT TWO Scene 3: Along a Leafy Lane
ACT TWO Scene 4: In the Pickins Saw Mill

GRUB GULCH GARTER GIRLS: Patti Law, Candy Earnest, Janis Goldman, Joyce Gilliland, Kathy Cable, DeLois Rose, Marcia Wilkins, Pat Kellogg, Sheila Wood.

GRUB GULCH GRANNIES: Grace Rabourn, Betty Smith, Bernie Dent, Betty Boltinhouse, Clemmie Woupio, Helen West.

GRUB GULCH GRANDADS: Bud Rabourn, Lee Smith, Ric Chipman, Frank Holterman, Jonny West, Jack Jines.

PRODUCED BY THE FOLLOWING
ENSEMBLE OF MAGNIFICENT AIDES

Choreographer .... Mrs. Patti Law
Technical Designer .... Mr. J. Frank Martin
Scenic Artists .... Mrs. Carol Savage, Mrs. Jane Gyer
Scenery Painters-Mrs. Betty Poteet, Mrs. Lucille Smith, Mrs. Josephine Barra
Costumes .... Mrs. DeLois Rose, Mrs. Martha Hess, Mrs. Betty Sturkey
Makeup and Hair Styling, ... Mrs. Janis Goldman, Mrs. LaRetta Roope
Sound and Lighting .... Mr. George Bushnell, Mr. Ted Kerber
Promptress .... Mrs. Betty Dick
Ushers .... Under the direction of Mrs. Dee Moody
Box Office .... Mrs. Agnes Carroll

119

120

UNIVERSITY THEATRE

C.S.U.F.

PROUDLY PRESENTS

WORLD PREMIERE

THE SORROWS OF SADIE

or "DOUBLE TROUBLE!"

by Charles H. Randall
and Joan LeGro Bushnell
October 4-5-6 and 9-10-11-12-13, 1979 8:15 P.M.
Matinee Sunday, October 7 at 2:00 P.M.
Arena Theatre

MR. CHARLES H. RANDALL'S Directorial Diligence has been Dedicated to Designing the Dazzling Demonstration of Dramatic Deportment Displayed by the Devoted Disciples of Drama. The Demands of the Debilitating Deed were Definately Decreased by Delegating Diverse Duties to the Delightful and Dedicated Deputy, **MISS KATHLEEN MC KINLEY. MISS MC KINLEY'S** mastery of the Manifold Mysteries of Management Maintained Momentum in the Manufacture of the Moments of Mirth and Masterminded the Miscellaneous Mid-Act Musical Merriment.

The stirring dramatic action takes place in the living room of the Haverford home in Philadelphia, Christmas, mid-1890's. The stunning scenic effects were designed by our own tremendously talented **MR. HOWARD BREWER.** The cleverly conceived costumes and marvelous make-up were masterminded by pretty **MISS PAMELA HUTH. MR. GREG ORTIZ** added the illuminating lighting.

When the curtain rises, the audience is requested to limit the duration of its expression of approbation in order to avoid excessive delay in the performance.

Boos, Hisses, and Cheers are encouraged. All Screams, however, will be investigated!

INTRODUCING THE ENSUING EXTRAORDINARY ENSEMBLE
(In The Order Of Appearance)
MRS. PATRICIA O'CONNOR as Grace Haverford, a Gracious Guardian Given to

DIRECTOR'S NOTE

Welcome to the world premiere of a new play in an old form. **THE SORROWS OF SADIE, or "DOUBLE TROUBLE!"** is presented in the mold of a kind of theatre popular during the latter half of the nineteenth century. In those days, before Hollywood or the television industry was around to shape the thinking of the masses, popular melodramas carried the torch of morality. In melodramas, good always prevailed after a series of harrowing encounters with consumate evil. Audiences took these dramatized sermons very seriously, and never hesitated to voice their disapproval of the villain's antics, to cheer the hero in his desperate struggle to conquer the forces of evil, or to weep for the plight of the beleaguered heroine. We hope you will join in the spirit of fun and let that cad know how much you abhor his underhanded dealings!

CH Randall

If you expect to rate as a gentlemen, do not expectorate on the floor.

Do not molest the lady next to you, She may BE a lady.

The audience is encouraged to participate in the lovely, lilting lyrics of the magical, musical melodies and stirring songs.

YOU TELL ME YOUR DREAM [I'll Tell You Mine]

Words by Semor Rice and Albert Brown   Music by Charles N. Daniels

You had a dream, Well I had one too.
I know mine's best 'cause it was of you.
Come, sweet heart, tell me, Now is the time.
You tell me your dream, I'll tell you mine.

THE YELLOW ROSE OF TEXAS

There's a yellow rose in Texas I'm going there to see,
No other fellow knows her, Nobody only me.
She cried so when I left her, It like to broke my heart,
and if we ever meet again, we never more shall part.
Refrain - 1st Verse
She's the sweetest rose of color, a fellow ever knew,
Her eyes are bright as diamonds, they sparkle like the dew.
You may talk about your dearest maids, and sing of Rosy Lee,
But **THE YELLOW ROSE OF TEXAS**, beats the belles of Tennessee.
(Where the) Rio Grande is flowing, Where stars are shining bright,
We walked along the river, on a quiet summer night.
She said if you remember, we parted long ago,
You promised to come back again and never leave me so.
Refrain - 2nd Verse
(Oh, I'm) going back to find her, my heart is full of woe,
we'll sing the songs together, we sang so long ago.
I'll pick the banjo gaily, and sing the songs of yore,
THE YELLOW ROSE OF TEXAS, she'll be mine forever more.
Refrain - 3rd Verse

IDA SWEET AS APPLE CIDER

Words by Eddie Leonard   Music by Eddie Munson

Ida! Sweet as apple cider.
Sweeter than all I know,
Come out! in the silvery moon light,
of love we'll whisper, so soft and low
Seems tho' can't live without you,
Listen oh! Honey do!
Ida! I idolize you
I love you, Ida, deed I do.

BILL BAILEY, WON'T YOU PLEASE COME HOME.

Hughie Cannon

On a summer day, sun was shining fine
Missus William Bailey was out hanging clothes on the line.
She and Bill had fussed, Bill had said good-bye.
All her neighbors felt so sorry when she started to cry -
Chorus
Won't you come home, Bill Bailey, won't you come home?
I miss you all the day long.
I'll do the cooking honey, I'll pay the rent;
I know I done you wrong.
'Member that rainey evening, I drove you out,
With nothing but a fine tooth comb?
I know I'm to blame, well ain't that a shame!
Bill Bailey **WON'T YOU PLEASE COME HOME?**

PRODUCTION STAFF

Stage Manager	Kathleen Mc Kinley
Assistant Stage Manager	Kia Mosley
Scene Shop Foreman	Floyd Skaggs
Master Carpenter	Bill Shoults
Scene Painters	Dan Carrion, Phil Douglas, Tom Wolfgang
Prop Manager	Kia Mosley
Stage and Prop Crew	Cindy Allen, Jeanette Beam, Claudia Cunha
Light Board Operators	Laura Humason, Mike Kissel
Lighting Crew	Kathryn Hansen, Laura Humason, Mike Kissel, Diane Printz
Costume Shop Supervisor	Anna Levin
Wardrobe Manager	Paula Balekian
Wardrobe Crew	Bruce Bower, Monica Silveria
Make-up Manager	Karen Hagerman
Make-up Crew	Tracy Douglas, Lora Tompkins
Box Office Managers	Marta Hagen, Susan Stump
House Manager	Susan Stump
House Crew	Christine Giannopoulous, Mary Glazier, Evelyn Murphy
Promotion	Philip Douglas, Tom Wolfgang, Sam Jenkins, Karen Holsenback, Larry Starrh, Kerry Smith, Thomas Hall

Gentlemen will please refrain from removing their boots.

GOLDEN CHAIN THEATRE

PROUDLY PRESENTS

1978's
ALL NEW SEASON!

OF ROLLICKING FUN-FILLED

MELODRAMS

An Authentic American Classic
Lillian Mortimer's

No Mother to Guide Her

* spectacular!
* Action packed!
* Thrilling!

OPENS JUNE 22
8:15 P.M.

see reverse side for complete
season schedule.

World Premiere!

MISS MELODY'S LAMENT

OR

Dirty Deeds on Deck!

AN EXPLOSIVE MELODRAMA

Book, Music and Lyrics
By
Joan LeGro Bushnell

Gala Premiere Aug. 3   8:15 P.M.

ENTICING REFRESHMENTS! DELIGHTFUL OLIO ENTERTAINMENT!

YES, We Want In On The FUN!

PLEASE RESERVE THE FOLLOWING TICKETS AT $4.00

No Mother
number of tickets To Guide Her   (date)

and/or

Miss Melody's
(number)   Lament   (date)

Note: If you wish your tickets mailed to you, please
include a stamped, self-addressed envelope. (Otherwise, tickets will be held for you at the Box Office.)

Individual Mail and Phone Reservations to be paid
1 week in advance of performance.

make checks payable to: GOLDEN CHAIN THEATRE

GOLDEN CHAIN THEATRE
P.O. Box 604
Oakhurst, Ca. 93644

NAME _____
(please print)

ADDRESS _____

CITY _____

PHONE _____

AMT. ENCLOSED _____

123

WELCOME!

Things are really humming as we make preparations for another exciting season of melodramas. We are convinced that this season, the start of our second decade, will even top 1977's record smashing success.

Because so many of our friends were turned away last year by the "sold out" sign, we have added an extra matinee performance for both "NO MOTHER" and "MISS MELODY".

We are especially excited at the prospect of another World Premiere - MISS MELODY'S LAMENT or Dirty Deeds on Deck! This brand new musical melodrama is the work of our own Joan LeGro Bushnell, co-author of last year's smash hit, Little Orphan Angela. We hope you will make your reservations early for both of these great new productions! Don't be left out!

BOARD OF DIRECTORS
GOLDEN CHAIN THEATRE

SEASON SCHEDULE

No Mother to Guide Her

SUN.	MON.	TUES.	WED.	THURS.	FRI.	SAT.
					June 22	June 23	June 24
					Sold Out	July 1
					Sold Out	July 8
		Matinee 2:30 P.M.			Sold Out	July 15
July 16					Sold Out	July 22
					July 28	July 29

Miss Melody's Lament

SUN.	MON.	TUES.	WED.	THURS.	FRI.	SAT.
				Aug. 3	Aug. 4	Aug. 5
					Sold Out	Aug. 12
					Aug. 18	Aug. 19
		Matinee 2:30 P.M.			Aug. 25	Aug. 26
Aug. 27					Sept. 1	Sept. 2
					Sept. 8	Sept. 9

SELECT YOUR DATES NOW!

MAIL YOUR RESERVATIONS TO:

GOLDEN CHAIN THEATRE

P.O. Box 604
Oakhurst, California 93644

Box Office Opens June 1st
Box Office Hours:
1 P.M. to 6 P.M.

CALL (209) 683-7112

Admission $4.00

☆ *Cabaret Style Seating*
☆ *Beer* - Soft Drinks - Popcorn

**1978 Season
June 22 thru Sept. 9**

FAMILY FUN!

Old fashioned melodramas are just plain old fashioned fun. As a member of our audience, you play a vital role in the production. The fun really takes off when you hiss and jeer at the despicable villain, and shake the rafters with cheers for the dashing hero! So get the gang together and come get in the act!

Call (209) 683-7112 now for your reservations for a delightful evening of old fashioned fun. You'll enjoy the show—and you'll enjoy the drive—just two easy miles north of Oakhurst on Highway 41.

AND

Groups of 25 or more may obtain tickets at a whopping discount! Get the gang together and come to the new GOLDEN CHAIN THEATRE for an evening of great family fun. Try this unique way to entertain your clients.
(Payable in full 10 days in advance). For details CALL (209) 683-7112 1 p.m. to 6 p.m.

Squirrel Cage Theatre
presents

****
3RD ANNUAL "GAY '90's REVUE"
****

Friday		Saturday
Sept. 23	Curtain	Sept. 24
Sept. 30	8:00 p.m.	Oct. 1

North Fork Town Hall — Admission $3.00

Squirrel Cage Theatre
presents

****
3RD ANNUAL "GAY '90's REVUE"
****

Friday   Saturday
Sept. 23   Curtain   Sept. 24
Sept. 30   8:00 p.m.   Oct. 1
North Fork Town Hall — Admission $3.00

Squirrel Cage Theatre
presents
3RD ANNUAL "GAY '90's REVUE"
Friday   Saturday
Sept. 23   Curtain   Sept. 24
Sept. 30   8:00 p.m.   Oct. 1
North Fork Town Hall — Admission $3.00

Squirrel Cage Theatre
presents
3RD ANNUAL "GAY '90's REVUE"
Friday   Saturday
Sept. 23   Curtain   Sept. 24
Sept. 30   8:00 p.m.   Oct. 1
North Fork Town Hall — Admission $3.00

Squirrel Cage Theatre
presents
3RD ANNUAL "GAY '90's REVUE"
Friday   Saturday
Sept. 23   Curtain   Sept. 24
Sept. 30   8:00 p.m.   Oct. 1
North Fork Town Hall — Admission $3.00

Squirrel Cage Theatre
presents
3RD ANNUAL "GAY '90's REVUE"
Friday   Saturday
Sept. 23   Curtain   Sept. 24
Sept. 30   8:00 p.m.   Oct. 1
North Fork Town Hall — Admission $3.00

Squirrel Cage Theatre
presents
3RD ANNUAL "GAY '90's REVUE"
Friday   Saturday
Sept. 23   Curtain   Sept. 24
Sept. 30   8:00 p.m.   Oct. 1
North Fork Town Hall — Admission $3.00

Squirrel Cage Theatre
presents
3RD ANNUAL "GAY '90's REVUE"
Friday   Saturday
Sept. 23   Curtain   Sept. 24
Sept. 30   8:00 p.m.   Oct. 1
North Fork Town Hall — Admission $3.00

Squirrel Cage Theatre
presents
3RD ANNUAL "GAY '90's REVUE"
Friday   Saturday
Sept. 23   Curtain   Sept. 24
Sept. 30   8:00 p.m.   Oct. 1
North Fork Town Hall — Admission $3.00

Squirrel Cage Theatre
presents
3RD ANNUAL "GAY '90's REVUE"
Friday   Saturday
Sept. 23   Curtain   Sept. 24
Sept. 30   8:00 p.m.   Oct. 1
North Fork Town Hall — Admission $3.00

Squirrel Cage Theatre
presents
3RD ANNUAL "GAY '90's REVUE"
Friday   Saturday
Sept. 23   Curtain   Sept. 24
Sept. 30   8:00 p.m.   Oct. 1
North Fork Town Hall — Admission $3.00

D. The Ushers

In addition to costumes, ushers should wear some other identifying feature such as straw hats or poke bonnets. The head usher takes tickets. If seats are numbered, half of the ticket is then turned over to another usher who will escort audience members to their seats. It's a good idea to have on hand a few small flashlights to guide the inevitable late arrivals!

E. The Seating

When possible, melodrama is at its best presented in a relaxed surrounding with cabaret-style seating to simulate the old music hall atmosphere. This surrounding is particularly easy to create in schools whose facilities combine cafeteria and stage. (Especially if you can drum up some red/white checkered plastic tablecovers!)

The California State University/Fresno production of *Trapped by a Treacherous Twin* was presented not on the main stage but in a smaller theatre with U-shape bleacher-style seating augmented by a few small tables and chairs down front.

When conditions permit, a sawdust-covered floor greatly adds to the effect.

F. The Refreshments

Popcorn and beer are traditional melodrama fare. Other snacks, such as peanuts, pretzels and soft drinks, may be served by waiters and waitresses in costume. Some groups serve hot dogs. It is, of course, necessary to obtain a license to sell any alcoholic beverage. Usually, such a permit (temporary) is obtainable through county offices. When beer is not permitted, root beer and sparkling cider may be substituted. If refreshments are sold, it's helpful to have a list on each table to let customers know what is available and at what prices. In the case of a limited budget, this price list may be included in the program.

In the case of a budget in people power, as previously suggested, the greeter may double as master or mistress of ceremonies. Ushers may distribute programs or the programs may be preset at tables or seats. If refreshments are offered only during intermission, ushers may double as servers. We believe, however, that it is better to keep these responsibilities separate, if at all possible.

It's often helpful to instruct ushers and servers to encourage audience participation by *hissing, booing* or *cheering* at appropriate moments during the entertainment.

In order to further establish the mood, it's a good idea for the piano player to render a medley of familiar songs of the Gay Nineties fifteen minutes or more before the curtain opens. The piano player and any other musicians should be in costume. Men may wear dark pants, long-sleeved shirts with garters, string ties, and vests. Ladies may wear long skirts with high-necked blouses suggestive of the Victorian era.

Okay! And, by the way, we *never* say "okay" in melodrama. (It's an anachronism!) Let's assume that your audience is seated and served, hopefully humming along with those old-time melodies. It's a giant step toward involvement! But what about those *hisses, boos* and *cheers* so integral to successful melodrama? In addition to being fun, these extra touches encourage the audience participation so important to the success of your melodrama.

G. The M.C.

The Master or Mistress of Ceremonies (M.C.) serves as the teacher who instructs your audience in how to react to melodrama. We call it a *warm-up* and we consider it essential to a successful melodrama production.

Many years ago when we attended our first melodrama, there was no M.C. to instruct or warm up the audience. There was no booing of the villain or cheering for the hero because hardly anybody in the audience understood what was expected. Those few who did know what to do were not able to draw a reaction from the rest of us, so conditioned were we to "regular" theatre. Like the turkey without its stuffing, there was definitely something missing. It was a memorable experience but not as enjoyable as it might have been, and it was ten years before we were coaxed into attending another melodrama!

Some productions feature their villain as M. C. We prefer to cast a *Mistress* of Ceremonies as a balance for the male villain. We see this female as a "Diamond Lil" type, dramatically dressed and draped in plenty of maribou and sparkle. When costumes are a problem, the M. C. may dress much like ushers, servers, or musicians.

As we've previously mentioned, some M. C.'s double as greeters. The obvious advantage in this is that the audience has already "met" the M. C. when he or she comes onstage and the feeling of familiarity is off to a head start. However, when there are enough people available, we prefer to keep these two roles separate. The more, the merrier in melodrama!

What is most important is that the M.C. have a good voice (singing as well as speaking), an outgoing personality, and the charisma to create and encourage rapport with the audience — in short, the gift of gab and the ability to project it!

All this is not as easy as it may sound. We have worked with numerous "Diamond Lils" (and "Dapper Dans") who, charming though they may be on the downstage side of the footlights, simply do not come across to a crowd. As anyone who has experienced the challenge knows, it takes a special expertise to address a large audience under ad lib conditions — even more to handle oneself and the audience as well! Thus, the role of M. C. should not be underestimated. As the link between cast and audience, the M. C. must project a love of people and an ability to reach and respond on an individual as well as on a collective basis. It is the M. C. who, more than anyone else, sets the pace of your show.

Important as the gift of gab or the ability to ad lib may be, we have found, as with the rest of the production, that the better part of showmanship is preparation. In addition to warming up the audience, an M. C. may have all manner of other information to give. Are there more performances? If so, when? Is someone substituting in a role? Has a name been left of the program? (Horrors!)

Notes carried onstage can be distracting both to the audience and the M. C. although sometimes they may be necessary. What works best, we find, is for the M. C. to memorize a loose format, then run through this just before going onstage.

If your theatrical conditions permit, an "olio curtain" can add yet another atmospheric frill to your fun and frolic. So called because it is used as a backdrop for "olio acts," between-the-scene entertainment (about which we'll learn more in a page or two), the olio curtain is not a conventional travelling curtain. It is, rather, a roll drop which hangs between the travellers and the proscenium arch.

Originally, the fire-proof asbestos curtain required by law served as an olio curtain and this remains the case in many modern-day theatres specifically designed for melodrama. For "one-shot" melodrama productions, an effective facsimile may be achieved by hanging a regular drop, if space or lack thereof dictates, just inside the travellers. Traditionally, this drop is painted with advertisements which may be real (another source of revenue) or tongue-in-cheek (another source of amusement). Often these ads, if contrived, feature the names of cast members, local citizens, or special people in the audience.

With the olio curtain in place and the M. C. waiting in the wings, it's showtime!

Accordingly, the piano switches from its old-time tunes to an opener. In addition to its current popularity, Scott Joplin's *The Entertainer* dates back to the days of melodrama. We have found this piece to work well both as a rousing conclusion to the pre-show medley and an unmistakeable cue for stage crew and M. C. Houselights fade as *The Entertainer* begins, and a spotlight is directed on the piano player who may take a bow at the end of the number.

The piano plays *Oh, You Beautiful Doll* or *For He's A Jolly Good Fellow* or any other such suitable theme for the M. C. as the olio curtain rises and the spotlight is directed on the M. C.'s entrance. If the M. C. uses a microphone (and we think this is a good idea), there will need to be a stagehand in the wings who is responsible for handing over the mike with *tangle-free* cord. There's plenty of opportunity for comedy in melodrama without an unrehearsed stumble which could be both distracting and dangerous!

M. C.: *Good evening, ladies and gentlemen, and welcome to "————!" Tonight's production is the (premiere?) performance of "————!" We have a wonderful show in store for you, and we'll be telling you more about this in just a moment. But first, while everyone's getting seated, why don't we start out with a song or two?* (Houselights up to half.) *You'll find songsheets on the backs of your programs. Why don't we start with "————?"* (Piano plays brief introduction to allow time to find songsheets.) *Ready? Set? Go!* (Piano plays intro again. Sing song.) *All right, now that we're getting into the mood, why don't we try it again, and let's really hear it this time!* (Piano plays intro then repeat song.) *You sound wonderful! Let's do another one! How about "————?"* (Piano plays intro. Sing song.) *You are good! Give yourselves a hand!* (Applause.) *I have a feeling this is going to be our best show ever!* (Explain how to get whatever refreshments may be available and any other performances which may be scheduled.) *Tell me, how many here have never seen a melodrama before?* (Houselights down.) *Well, you're in for a treat! You* *know, melodrama's a very special kind of entertainment and you, our audience, are a very special part of our show. In fact, we couldn't do the show without you because we need you to enter into all the excitement that takes place here onstage. That's right! We want <u>you</u> to be a part of our one, big, happy melodrama family! So . . . We're going to combine some introductions with a little practice session. Of course, we <u>know</u> you'll be polite, but <u>please</u> don't be <u>too quiet</u>! Are we ready?* (Piano plays *Charge Theme*.) *Good! For all of you who <u>have</u> seen melodrama before, who can tell me what we do when the villain comes onstage?* (Piano plays *Villain's Theme* as the villain sweeps through the curtain to snarl at the audience, then exits quickly with a flourish of his cape.) *Boo! Hiss! That's right! We need to let that bad actor know how nasty we think he is! Now, for the hero?* (Piano plays *Hero's Theme* as the hero enters to take a bow and fast exit.) *Yea! We cheer the hero! But for our heroine, poor little put-upon thing . . .* (Piano plays *Heroine's Theme* as the heroine enters to take a quick curtsey and exit. All entrances and exits should be snappy in order to keep the attention of the audience.) *Aw-ww-ww!* (Sigh.) *We <u>sigh</u> for the heroine because we feel so sorry for her. You sound so good at this that I can't believe <u>all</u> of you haven't done it before! I don't think you need any more coaching. I think you're ready for your show, so let's get on with it with the <u>Can-Can</u>!* (Run offstage as the piano begins Offenbach's *Can-Can* and Can-Can dancers run on.)

H. The Dancing Girls

Many melodramas begin with a line of dancing girls which executes a lively Can-Can immediately preceding the opening curtain of the play. This selection of terpsichoral pulchritude in colorful costume is invariably an excellent means of warming up an audience. Offenbach's *Can-Can* music accompanied by the traditional whoops of the dancers should encourage a spirited response with even more to follow for the tossing of the dancers' garters at the conclusion of the number.

For the troupe with a limited budget (and aren't they all!), Can-Can costumes are easily assembled from several ruffled petticoats under knee-length black skirts worn with red camisole tops. Red panties and black fishnet hose complete the basic costume. Further effect is achieved with plumes worn in the hair and neckbands with flowers on them. Inexpensive garters may be purchased in novelty stores. If dancing shoes are unavailable, black medium-heel pumps may be found in closets and second-hand shops. A word to the wise: It's a good idea to secure these pumps with black elastic band lest an overly-enthusiastic kick direct a shoe into a basket of popcorn — and we've seen it happen!

As the Can-Can dancers run offstage, the piano begins a passage of incidental music and the curtain opens on Act I, Scene 1!

I. The Olio

Once the play is underway, next in the order of melodrama tradition is the *olio* (o-leo). Deriving from the Spanish *olla* meaning pot or stew, melodrama olios are brief acts, a potpourri of period songs, dances, or comical sketches, featured before the curtain or in designated areas.

Some directors present olio acts as an independent introduction to the melodrama while others feature them as a separate segment following an intermission at the end of the play. The latter treatment is particularly effective with a one-act play. Because we work primarily with full-length, two or three-act scripts, in keeping with the more common treatment of the olio, we prefer to play these selections between scenes in order to allow time for a change of set without a change of pace, thus assuring a smoother production.

When it comes to choosing olio material, the opportunities are extensive. Many less familiar songs, not so suitable as incidental music, are smash hits when used as olio acts. Stunt books, available in most public libraries, are sometimes a good source. Recitations of poetry and monologues, both comical and dramatic, were common to the 1800's. We prefer, however, not to use dialogues in olios since we believe songs, dances, and pantomime present a more pleasing contrast to the spoken word of the melodramatic play.

Pantomime in melodramatic theatre was a form of comedy in which the performers expressed themselves through silent gestures, rather than words, to the accompaniment of incidental music. A look at some of the routines made famous by Charlie Chaplin can provide a variety of olio sources.

Parody or burlesque, as it was known in nineteenth-century theatre, was also popular as an "afterpiece" or "Comedietta" following the dramatic play. Presented as satire, such burlesque often mocked the more serious work which preceded it. The purpose of this was, no doubt, the ever-constant performers' desire to "leave 'em laughin'!"

Circus-type performers who practiced balancing and tumbling were popular entr'acte entertainment in early nineteenth-century theatre. The Ravel family, an acrobatic troup, travelled as a complete company from theatre to theatre across the country. In addition to dogs, equestrian troups were featured on theatre stages along with elephants, zebras, and apes! Magic acts were in demand and a "Mr. Rannie," who specialized in replacing the severed head of a rooster, was a star performer.

Many critics of the day found fault with these pieces of entertainment, complaining that they were not appropriate to the serious theatrical endeavors which surrounded them. Popular demand, however, won out. It wasn't until the latter half of the nineteenth century that the theatre-goer's taste turned to opera and ballet, and such novelty acts found a permanent place in the circus tents of P. T. Barnum.

Barbershop quartets were extremely popular during the late 1800's and are equally well-received today. Minstrel songs also comprised a major portion of the popular music of the Gay Nineties and the songs of Stephen Foster were much-loved.

Some directors like to choose olio material whose contents complement a play, either by being in keeping with or in contrast to the play's theme. As in that stew composed of numerous ingredients or the potpourri, unless we have a most fitting choice in mind for a particular point in the show, we prefer to ask performers to choose and prepare their own olio material to be auditioned shortly after the melodrama has been cast. Often this results in a new and fresh supply of olio material.

Although it is perfectly appropriate to have olios performed by members of the cast, there is a certain advantage to using others to perform these acts. This allows more people to become part of the production while requiring less rehearsal time for the regular cast. Also, it's often a good way to smooth the ruffled feathers of that songbird who wasn't quite right for the role of the heroine, but who is certain to excel in an olio act!

An important factor to bear in mind in the choice and preparation of olio material is that these pieces are meant to augment a production, not to overshadow it. They should, therefore, be carefully timed in order to be most effective. We cannot stress strongly enough that all music and other material used in conjunction with melodrama should be taken from the period spanning or prior to the Gay Nineties and early 1900's when this style was at its peak. Anything from a later period is anachronistic and, therefore, inappropriate. It's also good to remember never to underestimate the integrity of your audience, the albeit silent majority of which will surely recognize that number from the "Roarin' Twenties" which simply does not fit!

A selection of songs suitable for olios will be identified in the list of music at the end of this section.

We have used vocal solos, duets and quartets, dance routines which included audience participation, animal acts, harp, guitar, and piano selections — even Scottish bagpipes! We once used a "magic lantern" to project antique glass slides on the curtain. Variety is truly the spice of that mixture known as olio entertainment!

Boo-oo-oo! The piano plays an appropriate passage of incidental music as the curtain closes on the final scene of Act I, presumably one in which the villain triumphs — for the moment, at least. The piano then segues to girlie-type music as a dancing girl glides across the stage carrying an "Intermission" sign. Suddenly, the piano plays the *Villain's Theme* and the villain enters to pursue the girl in exaggerated stealth. About two-thirds of the way across the stage, the girl looks back — responding to the warnings of the audience — sees the villain, screams, and runs offstage with the villain in hot pursuit. House-lights are brought up for intermission.

J. The Souvenir

Getting back to those throw-away garters tossed to the audience by the Can-Can dancers, there are bound to be others who would like such a souvenir of the evening's entertainment. A good source of revenue to help cover production expenses is the sale of same during intermission by dancers in Can-Can costume. Also available in novelty shops are moustaches which make equally good souvenirs to be sold from vendors' trays, cardboard boxes cut down or beverage cases, covered, and suspended by cord from the vendors' shoulders.

K. The Intermission

At the end of the intermission (timed and signaled by the stage manager), the piano plays a chorus of the *M. C.'s Theme* to alert the audience. At the beginning of the second chorus, the M. C. runs onstage. This is the time for a jaunty gait and a snappy delivery!

Just as the prime function of an M. C. is to warm up the audience before the show starts, so must the M. C. get the audience back in the mood following intermission.

M. C.: (Houselights down.) *Are you having a good time?* (Hopefully, applause.) *Good! That's what we're here for! How about another song while everyone's getting seated again?* (Houselights up half.) *Remember those song-sheets on the backs of your programs? Let's sing "———!"* (The piano plays intro again and all sing song.) *One more time!* (Sing song again.) *You're a wonderful audience! And you sound wonderful! And you know why you sound so good? It's all because of the marvelous music by* (mention the piano player and the other musicians)! *Let's give (him, her, them) a big hand!* (The piano player takes a bow and acknowledges other musicians, if any. Houselights down while any other necessary announcements are made. Some productions feature the drawing of a prize or prizes which have been donated by local merchants in return for credit on your program or olio curtain. Chances may be sold before the show and during intermission or may be chosen by ticket number. This is the moment for the big drawing!) *And now, without further adieu, it's time to get on with the exciting conclusion of "———!"* (Run offstage as the piano begins passage of incidental music and the curtain opens on Act II.)

If your play calls for more than one intermission, the format is the same with a part of the preceding spread out over the M. C.'s third appearance. The only difference is that the villain will *catch* the intermission girl, throw her over his shoulder, and carry her away — offstage, that is.

A warning note: No matter how carefully we may prepare, there are times when there may be unexpected delays. An M. C. should be ready for such emergencies with an extra song to lead and a backup musical round to teach the audience. Rounds can be wonderful stallers for time since they may go on indefinitely (fate forbid!) until a signal of flashing lights cues that *the show will go on!*

Just in case all of these "in cases" seem picayune, any director whose show

134

has come to an unexpected and seemingly endless halt will attest that, wherever possible, it is better to be prepared than penitent!

Yea-ea-ea! Finally, the villain is brought to justice. The hero and his heroine are reunited. All's well that ends well, but it's not over yet.

L. The Curtain Call

Quick, quick, quick! With the final curtain, the piano segues from the last passage of incidental music to a rousing curtain call number. If the play is a musical, a song from the score should be used and the company may sing. Otherwise, any appropriate period song will work as long as it is lively. This is the moment to take full advantage of audience reaction. With the curtain closed and while the applause still rings, dancers, olio entertainers, the M. C., extras and chorus march onstage — from right to left if possible — to take a collective bow, then part right and left to make room for the cast. Beginning with the minor principal roles in order of their importance, cast members enter at center, through the curtain, to take individual bows and move right and left to make room for the hero, the heroine, and the traditional final bow which belongs to the villain.

This business *must* move fast in order to avoid a lull in the applause. There's no greater letdown than a slow or sloppy curtain call. Like every other little detail in theatre, the curtain call should not be underestimated. It is the final memory the audience will carry and, therefore, should be every bit as entertaining as your show.

The full company then takes a bow and all but the principals march off right and left. The curtain opens and the principals take another bow together, then step back above the curtain line as the curtain closes. If you're good enough to have them still applauding, the curtain will open for yet another bow. Never, *never*, however, attempt to "milk the call" or go for another curtain call when audience reaction is dwindling. This kind of know-how takes a good ear for applause and careful timing on the part of the curtain puller, as the idea is to leave on a high note, not a dead beat!

M. The Lineup

Some melodrama theatres follow the practice of lining up the cast in the lobby or in the rear of the auditorium to meet the audience as it leaves. Especially for amateur groups, this provides more recognition for all that hard work. In every group, it provides audience members more of that rapport with the company that is truly the fun of melodrama.

And this *is* what melodrama is all about today. Still theatre for the people after almost two centuries, this classic form continues to endure and continues to be fun!

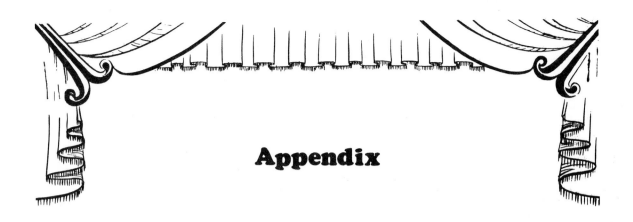

Appendix

A. A Selection of Published Melodramas

Adrift in New York by Addison Aulger.
Full-length with optional music. 9m., 6f., extras.
Dramatic Publishing Company

Adrift in New York. Book, lyrics and music by Robert Neil Porter
and Jack Perry.
About 90 mins. 5m., 8f., extras, chorus. Simple int.
Pioneer Drama Service

Because Their Hearts Were Pure (or The Secret of the Mine) by Morland Cary.
Full-length. 6m., 9f., extras. Several simple ints. and exts.
Dramatists Play Service

Bertha, The Bartender's Beautiful Baby by Charles George.
A short play. 4m., 5f. Simple int.
Dramatists Play Service

Bertha, The Beautiful Typewriter Girl by Charles George.
Three-act. 5m., 5f., int.
Baker's Plays

Caught in the Villain's Web (or More Sinned Against Than Sinning) by Herbert
E. Swayne.
Full-length. 4m., 6f., int.
Samuel French, Inc.

Curse of an Aching Heart (or Trapped in the Spider's Web) by Herbert E. Swayne.
Three-act. 4m., 7f., int.
Samuel French, Inc.

Curse You, Jack Dalton by Wilbur Braun.
One-act. 3m., 4f., int.
Samuel French, Inc.

Deadwood Dick (or A Game of Gold) by Tom Taggart.
Three-act. 7m., 7f., extras, int.
Baker's Plays

Desperate Desperadoes at Coyote Gulch by Snead Hearn.
One-act. 2m., 2f. One set.
Performance Publishing Company

Dirty Work at the Crossroads by Bill Johnson.
Three-act. 3m., 7f., ext.
Samuel French, Inc.

Dora, The Beautiful Dishwasher (or The Heroine Who Cleaned Up!) by Ned Albert.
One-act. 3m., 4f., int.
Samuel French, Inc.

Drunkard by Raymond Hull.
Two-act. 3m., 2f. 2 hours. Simple drops.
Pioneer Drama Service

Drunkard. Book, lyrics and music by Brian J. Burton.
7m., 8f. Multiple settings.
Samuel French, Inc.

Drunkard (or The Fallen Saved) by William H. Smith.
Five-act. 13m., 5f. Various int. and ext.
Samuel French, Inc.

East Lynne by Brian J. Burton.
Full-length. 4m., 5f.
Samuel French, Inc.

East Lynne by Ned Albert.
Full-length. 5m., 8f., int.
Samuel French, Inc.

East Lynne, a mellow musical adapted by Robert Neil Porter and Jack Perry.
5m., 10f. 2 hours. One basic set.
Pioneer Drama Service

Gaslight Girl. Music by Claire Strauch. Book and lyrics by John Jakes.
Full-length. 6m., 4f., plus chorus which plays bit parts.
Dramatic Publishing Company

Gold in the Hills (or The Dead Sister's Secret) by J. Frank Davis.
Three-act. Speaking: 13m., 7f., 1 child. Non-speaking: 5m., 4f., 3 singers, 1 pianist. 2 ints.
Baker's Plays

Hawkshaw, the Detective by Tim Kelly.
5m., 6f. 2 hours. Three simple int. sets.
Pioneer Drama Service

How the West Was Fun by James L. Seay.
Three-act. 5m., 7f., extras. One int.
Performance Publishing Company

Jenny, the Mail-Order Bride by Rosemary Fair.
Two-acts. 3m., 3f. 2 hours. Several simple sets.
Pioneer Drama Service

Lily, the Felon's Daughter by Tom Taggart.
Full-length. 5m., 6f. int.
Samuel French, Inc.

Little Nell, the Orphan Girl (or A Fight for a Woman's Honor!) by Nelson Goodhue.
Three-act. 4m., 8f., int.
Baker's Plays

Little Orphan Angela (or The Magician's Dirty Tricks!). Book by Charles H. Randall and Joan LeGro Bushnell. Lyrics and music by Joan LeGro Bushnell.
Two-act. 5m., 3f., flexible chorus.
Dramatic Publishing Company

Logger's Lament. Book and lyrics by Claire M. Resseger. Music by Helen Sanderson.
Full evening. 12m., 16f., flexible with extras, chorus. Representational sets.
Performance Publishing Company

Lost in the City (or The Triumph of Nellie) by Matthew O'Reilley.
Full evening. 9m., 13f., extras. Representational sets.
Performance Publishing Company

Love Rides the Rails (or Will the Mail Train Run Tonight?) by Morland Cary.
Full-length. 7m., 5f., extras. Several sets.
Dramatists Play Service

Millie, the Beautiful Working Girl (or Pursued by a Monstrous Villain) by Alec Tyson.
3m., 4f. 3 mins. One int. set.
Pioneer Drama Service

No Mother to Guide Her (or More to be Pitied Than Censured) by Alan Forsythe.
Three-act. 5m., 8f., int.
Baker's Plays

No Opera at the Op'ry House Tonight by Tim Kelly.
Full-length. 5m., 6f.
Dramatic Publishing Company

Perils of Priscilla (or The Schoolmarm's Dilemma) by Shubert Fendrick.
3m., 4f., extras. 30 mins. One int. set.
Pioneer Drama Service

Pure as the Driven Snow (or A Working Girl's Secret) by Paul Loomis.
Full-length. 5m., 8f., optional extras. One int. set.
Samuel French, Inc.

Sarsaparilla, Please. Book, lyrics and music by R. Cornelius Peters.
Full-length. 3m., 3f., pianist.
Dramatic Publishing Company

She Was Only a Farmer's Daughter by Millard Crosby.
3m., 5f., 30 mins. One int. set.
Baker's Plays

Showdown at the Rainbow Ranch.   Book by Charles H. Randall.   Music
and lyrics by Joan LeGro Bushnell.
Full-length. 4m., 4f.
Dramatic Publishing Company

Showdown at the Sugarcane Saloon.   Book and lyrics by Joseph Robinette.
Music by James R. Shaw.
Full-length. 5m., 5f.
Dramatic Publishing Company

Streets of New York.   Book by Barry A. Grael. Music by Richard B. Chodosh.
8m., 7f., chorus. Cyc. and latticework frame.
Samuel French, Inc.

Streets of New York (or The Poor of New York) by Dion Boucicault.
Five-act. 9m., 4f.
Samuel French, Inc.

Sweeney Todd, the Barber by Brian J. Burton.
Full-length. 11m., 5f., extras. Various drops.
Samuel French, Inc.

Ten Nights in a Bar-room by William W. Pratt.
Full-length. 7m., 4f. 4 ints. and 2 exts.
Samuel French, Inc.

Ten Nights in a Bar-room by Fred Carmichael.
(Musical comedy.) 7m., 4f., 1 boy, chorus of 3m., 4f.
Samuel French, Inc.

Trapped by a Treacherous Twin (or Double Trouble!!) by Charles H. Randall
and Joan LeGro Bushnell.
Two-act. 4m., 4f., int.
Dramatic Publishing Company

Virtue Victorious by Tim Kelly.
Full-length. 5m., 6f.
Dramatic Publishing Company

Wild Flowering of Chastity (or Chaste Across the Stage) by Dutton Foster.
One-act. 4m., 4f.
Dramatic Publishing Company

Sweeney Todd, the Demon Barber of Fleet Street by C. G. Bond.
Full-length. 8m., 3f. Various simple ints. and exts.
Samuel French, Inc.

B. Music Sources

The American Treasury of Golden Oldies Songbook
Compiled by Sandy King.
Charles Hansen, Inc., New York

America's Story in Song
Edited by Ronny Schiff.
Warner Brothers Publications, Inc.

Collegiate Song Book
M. M. Cole Publishing Company, Chicago

"88" Grand Old Songs
Edited by Elliott Shapiro. Arranged by Eugene Platzman.
Shapiro, Bernstein and Company, Inc., New York

Favorite Songs of the Nineties
Edited by Robert A. Fremont.
Dover Publications, Inc., New York

Fireside Book of Love Songs
Selected and edited by Margaret Bradford Boni.
Simon and Schuster, New York
Copyright 1954.

Flashes of Merriment; A Century of Humorous Songs in America, 1805–1905
Lester S. Levy
University of Oklahoma, 1971

"Gentlemen, Be Seated!" A Parade of the American Minstrels
Dailey Paskman
Clarkson N. Potter, Inc., New York, 1976

The Golden Book of Favorite Songs
Schmitt, Hall and McCreary Company, Minneapolis

Henry Clay Work Songs
Da Capo Press, New York

Jerry Silverman's Folk Song Encyclopedia, Volume I
Edited by Beverly Tillett.
Chappell Music Company, New York

The Legal Fake Book, Revised Edition
Warner Brothers Publications, Inc., 1979

Let Us Have Music for Piano in Two Volumes
Volume I, *Seventy-four Famous Melodies*
Arranged and edited by Maxwell Eckstein.
Carl Fischer, Inc., New York

Let Us Have Music for Piano in Two Volumes
Volume II, *Sixty-nine Famous Melodies*
Arranged and edited by Maxwell Eckstein.
Carl Fischer, Inc., New York

More Favorite Songs of the Nineties
Edited by Paul Charosh and Robert A. Fremont.
Dover Publications, Inc., New York

Motion Picture Moods for Pianists and Organists
Arranged by Erno Rapee.
G. Schirmer, Inc., New York

Folk Songs in Settings by Master Composers
Herbert Haufrecht
Funk and Wagnalls, New York
Copyright 1970

The Parlour Song Book
Edited by Michael R. Turner.
The Viking Press, New York

Sixty Patriotic Songs of All Nations
Edited by Granville Bantock.
Oliver Ditson Company, Boston

Songs of the Great American West
Compiled and edited by Irwin Silber.
The Macmillan Company, New York

A Treasury of American Song
Olin Downes and Elie Siegmeister, Second Edition.
Alfred A. Knopf, New York
Copyright 1943

Weep Some More, My Lady
Sigmund Spaeth
Doubleday, Page and Company, New York

World's Favorite Sing-Along Songs of the Gay Nineties
Selected and arranged by Albert Gamse.
Ashley Publications, Inc., New Jersey

C. Music References

They All Sang
by Edward B. Marks as told to Abbott J. Liebling.
The Viking Press, New York, 1935

Tin Pan Alley in Gaslight
Maxwell F. Marcuse
Century House, Watkins Glen, New York
Copyright 1959

Victorian Popular Music
Ronald Pearsall
Gale Research Company, Detroit
Copyright 1973

D. Regional Melodrama Theatres

ALASKA

Haines. Chikat Center for the Arts. Port Chilkat. (907) 766-2540 or (907) 766-2801.

Skagway. The Eagle's Hall Theatre. Broadway at Sixth Street. (907) 983-2545 or (907) 983-2234.

ARIZONA

Flagstaff. Black Bart's Old West Theatre. 2760 East Butler Avenue. (602) 779-3142.

Phoenix. The Sundown Stage Company at the Pioneer Arizona Living History Museum on Pioneer Road. 12 miles north of Phoenix via Interstate 17. (602) 993-0212.

Sedona. Memory Lane Theatre. Highway 89A. (602) 282-7722 or (602) 782-7735.

Tucson. The Gaslight Theatre. 7000 East Tanque Verde Road. (602) 885-9428.

CALIFORNIA

Auburn. The Old Town Troupers. Old Opera House Dinner Theater. 111 Sacramento Street. (916) 885-7708.

Bakersfield. The Great American Melodrama. 206 China Grade Loop. Oceano-based troupe. (See Oceano listing.) (805) 392-1900.

Buena Park. The Bird Cage Theatre at Knott's Berry Farm. (714) 827-1776.

Campbell. The Gaslight Theatre. 400 East Campbell Avenue. (408) 866-1408.

Drytown. The Claypipers. On State Highway 49, 10 miles north of Jackson. (415) 341-8991 100-year-old theatre. Saturday eves., June-September.

Monterey. California's First Theater. Part of Monterey State Historic Park. 1118 Piedmont Avenue, Pacific Grove. (408) 375-4916.

Oakhurst. The Golden Chain Theater. On Highway 41, 2 miles north of Oakhurst. (209) 683-7112. Friday and Saturday eves, June-Sept. Some Sunday matinees. Olios, sing-alongs, cabaret seating, refreshments.

Oceano. The Great American Melodrama. 1827 Pacific Blvd. (805) 489-2499.

San Jose. Old Op'ry House.

Santa Rosa. The Marque Theatre. 15 West Third Street. Railroad Square freight warehouse. (707) 545-1906.

Stockton. The Palace Showboat Dinner Theatre. 10464 North Highway 99. (209) 931-0274.

COLORADO

Cascade. Bob Young's Cabaret. Highway 24. (303) 684-9236.

Cripple Creek. The Imperial Hotel. 123 North Third Street. (303) 689-2713. Twelve-week summer season with one play adapted from the 1850-1900 period.

Durango. The Diamond Circle Theatre. Strater Hotel. 699 Main Avenue. (303) 247-4431.

IDAHO

Victor. Pierre's Playhouse. Highway 33. (208) 787-2249.

MONTANA

Virginia City. The Virginia City Players. Old Opera House. Wallace Street. (406) 843-5377.

West Yellowstone. The Playmill Theatre. 29 Madison Avenue. (406) 646-7757.

OREGON

Coquille. The Sawdust Theatre. Second and Adams Streets. (503) 396-4563.

Jacksonville. The Pioneer Village Melodrama. 725 North Fifth Street. (503) 899-1683.

Talent. Gilded Cage Players, Inc. 101 Talent Avenue, P.O. Box 353. (503) 535-5250.

NEW HAMPSHIRE

Tamworth. The Barnstormers. Francis G. Cleveland. (603) 323-8500.

Swanzey Center. The Old Homestead. Potash Bowl, Route 32, East Swanzey.

E. Glossary

Above. A position or movement upstage or further from the audience.

Act Curtain. The theatre's main curtain.

Acting. The creation of a dramatic characterization through the use of voice and movement.

Action. Onstage events projected by actors. The movement and business of an actor.

Ad-lib. Words or actions not called for by the script. Usually spontaneous additions during performance.

Antagonist. The character who most directly opposes the wishes of the hero or heroine. The villain!

Apron (also called forestage). That part of the stage area between the act curtain and the audience.

Apron Scene. Scene played on the apron, usually below a closed act curtain during a scene change.

Aside. A speech intended to be heard by the audience but not by other characters onstage.

Backdrop. A large cloth hanging at the rear of the set, painted to depict a locale.

Backstage. Behind the scenes, out of the sight of the audience.

Below. Nearer the audience. The opposite of above.

Blackout. The abrupt and total elimination of stage lights. Also a brief humorous skit punctuated by a blackout.

Blocking. The director's process of determining where and when actors move on the stage.

Body Position. The position of the actor's body in relation to the audience.

Border. A drop or curtain hung overhead, parallel to the footlights, used to conceal rigging and light sources in the stage house.

Box Set. An interior setting, usually realistic, consisting of three walls and, often, a ceiling.

Build. To add tension or heighten the emotional key of a scene, speech or action.

Bull Roarer. A simple sound effect device made from a tin can and a string or wire. Excellent for effects such as a creaking door.

Burlesque. A very broad, exaggeratedly low-comedy manner of playing.

Call Board. A backstage bulletin board on which notices for cast and crew are posted. It is generally required that all personnel check the call board daily.

Casting. The process of selecting the performers who will appear in a production.

Character Roles. Parts which rely on special traits such as age, social or mental status.

Chraracter Themes. Special incidental music played to identify a particular character.

Characterization. The actor's personification of a role.

Claque. Person or persons hired to sit in the audience and clap or laugh during a performance. An occasionally appropriate aid in encouraging audience responses in a melodrama.

Climax. The point of maximum plot complication or dramatic tension in a play or scene. Usually the turning point preceding the resolution.

Closed Turn. A stage turn executed in such a way that the actor's back is turned to the audience during the turn. The opposite of an open turn.

Company. The personnel of an organization producing a play. The cast and crew of a production.

Cover. To interfere with the audience's view of an actor or a piece of business. Sometimes intentional as in the case of fight scenes or stage violence. When unintentional, it detracts from the effectiveness of the moment.

Cross. Movement from one place on the stage to another or to pass in front of (below) another character.

Cue. A predetermined signal to an actor or stagehand for the next speech, action or effect to take place.

Cue Sheet. A written list of all cues for entrances, curtains and technical effects. Usually prepared and used by the stage manager.

Curtain Call. The appearance of the entire cast immediately after the final curtain to acknowledge the audience's applause.

Curtain Line. An imaginary line on the stage at the point where the curtain touches the floor. Also the final line of dialogue which cues the curtain.

Denouement. The final resolution of the plot. "Untying the knot." The end of a play following the climax.

Dialogue. The exchange of speeches by characters in a play.

Downstage. Toward or nearer to the audience. The opposite of upstage.

Dress Rehearsal. One or more of the final rehearsals which are conducted as though they were performances.

Drop. A piece of scenery which can be raised (flown) or lowered (dropped). Usually painted canvas.

Ellipsoidal Reflector. A spotlight which produces a sharp-edged beam. It is equipped with shutters which allow precise shaping of the beam of light. Often referred to by the trade name Leko.

Emotional Key. The degree of emotional tension of a play, a scene or a character.

Exit Line. The line of dialogue delivered by an actor just prior to leaving the stage.

Exposition. That part of a play in which the playwright supplies necessary information about what has gone on before the beginning of the play.

Farce. Low comedy based upon an exaggerated premise. Usually with very broadly drawn characters and physical action designed to elicit boisterous laughter.

Flat. A unit of scenery. A framed canvas on which is painted scenic representation.

Floodlight. A lighting instrument producing a broad spread of light. It cannot be focused.

Floor Plan (also called a ground plan). A scale drawing of the stage setting as it would appear from overhead.

Footlights. A row of low wattage lamps placed at the front edge of the stage. Now largely obsolete except for special circumstances such as the historic significance in staging an old-fashioned melodrama.

Fourth Wall. An imaginary wall completing a box set.

French Scene. A unit of play construction named for the French Neo-Classicists' practice of designating the entrance or exit of a character. That part of a play in which a single set of characters appear.

Front (also called front of the house). That part of the theatre which is available to and used by the audience.

Gelatin (usually shortened to gel). Colored transparencies used to add color to light from a stage instrument.

Gesture. Movement of hands, arms, shoulders or the head. Refers to use of a part of the body as opposed to the movement of the entire body.

Ground Plan. See floor plan.

Hold. To suspend dialogue or action for laughter or applause.

Houselights. All the auditorium lights except "exit" lights.

Improvising. Adding a bit of dialogue or piece of business which has not been predetermined in rehearsal. Acting without rehearsal.

Incidental Music. Background music. Used in melodrama either to identify characters or underscore the emotional content of a scene.

Justification. The reason for a character's action or speech. Also called motivation or objective.

Left or Right Stage. The left or right of an actor facing the audience.

Light Plot. A chart showing the placement of all lighting instruments, their cues and changes for the production.

Melodrama. In general, a play featuring suspense, excitement and physical action. In this book, a play simulating the style of popular theatre of the late nineteenth century.

Motivation. See justification.

Movement, Stage. Movement from one place on the stage to another. Distinct from stage business.

Olio. A variety of light musical entertainment traditionally presented with melodrama — either between acts or immediately after the final curtain.

Open. Turning or playing more directly toward the audience.

Overplay. To give unacceptable exaggeration to dialogue or action.

Pick Up. To speed up. Usually referring to cue pick-up or shortening the space between the cue and the following speech or action.

Presentational Staging. Non-realistic staging which recognizes the dual entities of the performers and the audience, making no effort to represent objective reality.

Production Meetings. Organizational meetings early in the production process usually conducted by the director. Meetings in which the director and all principal collaborators arrive at a common understanding of the style and methodology to be used in the production.

Properties (also called props). Any moveable object onstage except scenery. Large or fixed objects such as furniture are called *stage props*. Smaller objects which are handled by the actors are called *hand props*. A hand prop used by an individual actor — cigarette lighter, cane, etc. — is called a *personal prop.*

Proscenium. The architectural arch which frames the stage and separates it from the front of the house.

Protagonist. The central figure of a play, usually the hero whose struggle constitutes the basic plot. The opposite of the antagonist or villain.

Rain Machine. A narrow cylinder containing dried peas or buckshot. When rotated, it produces a sound like falling rain.

Realism. A style of production which attempts to create the illusion that the events depicted are actually happening for the first time.

Rehearsal. The process of preparing for performance.

Representational Staging. Staging which strives for realism.

Run-Through. A rehearsal in which a scene, act or entire play is gone through without interruption.

Scenario. An outline of the action of a play.

Scene. A segment of a play indicated by lowering the curtain or lights and denoting a change of place or time. Also, informally, an event or episode such as the "fight scene" or the "chase scene." See also French scene.

Sight Line. The line of sight from any seat in the auditorium to the stage. In common usage, the line of sight from the most extreme seats such as front sides or the back of the balcony.

Situational Themes. Incidental music selected to appropriately heighten the emotional key of specific situations.

Skit. A short dramatic episode, usually humorous. Sometimes used as olio entertainment.

Snow Machine. A long, narrow trough or cradle with a large-mesh screen as a bottom. It is filled with gypsum or other artificial snow and suspended overhead outside a window or door opening. The cradle is rigged with ropes so that it can be gently rocked to create falling "snow."

Spotlight. A lighting instrument that can be focused on a limited area.

Stage Business. Any action not involving crossing from one place to another.

Stage Manager. The director's principal aid during rehearsals and the individual responsible for coordinating and supervising all stage activities during performances.

Style. The technique or manner in which an act is performed or a play is produced.

Suspense. Sustained and heightened anticipation and uncertainty. A prime ingredient in melodrama.

Tag Line. The final line of dialogue before an exit or a curtain. Usually given extra emphasis through volume, tempo or accompanying gesture.

Teaser. A cloth border hung just upstage of the house curtain and below the tormentors. Used to mask the flies, ropes and lighting equipment.

Technique. The methodology by which a role or a play is communicated to an audience.

Telescope. To overlap speeches in picking up cues.

Theatricality. The sometimes distorted and always larger-than-life version of reality.

Throw-Away. To de-emphasize or underplay a line. Sometimes a deliberate technique to gain effect by contrast.

Thunder Sheet. A large rectangular sheet of tin or galvanized iron suspended backstage. When shaken, it produces an effective sound of thunder.

Topping. Capping a cue line by increased volume.

Tormentors. A pair of flats or drapes placed at both sides of the stage, just upstage of the proscenium. Used to mask the offstage areas and to adapt the width of the playing area.

Trap. An opening in the stage floor through which actors may enter from beneath the stage or use as an exit.

Turn In. To face or step toward center stage.

Turn Out. To face or step away from center stage.

Uncover. To move from behind another actor or a piece of furniture. Also to open or turn a piece of business so that the audience may see it.

Understudy. An actor who rehearses a role in order to be able to step in in the event the assigned actor should be unable to perform.

Upstage. Further from the audience. The opposite of downstage.

Wind Machine. A hand-cranked drum or cylinder over which is draped a piece of canvas. When rotated, it produces very effective sounds of a wind storm.

Wings. Offstage spaces at the sides of the playing area. Also flats or drapes used in pairs at the sides of the playing area to mask the offstage space.

Wing and Drop Setting. A setting which defines the playing area with several pairs of wings and a backdrop. An authentic setting for melodramas.

X. An actor's shorthand notation meaning "cross."

F. Bibliography

Burke, James and Nolan, Paul T.
Between Hisses, A Book of Songs and Olios for Melodrama
Second Edition
Pioneer Drama Service, Denver, Colorado, 1977

Charosh, Paul and Fremont, Robert A.
More Favorite Songs of the Nineties
Dover Publications, Inc., New York

Gassner, John
Producing the Play
Dryden Press, New York, 1941

Grimsted, David
Melodrama Unveiled, American Theater and Culture 1800-1850
University of Chicago Press, Chicago, London, 1968

King, Sandy
American Treasury of GOLDEN OLDIES Songbook
Charles Hansen, Inc., New York

Mackin, Dorothy
Melodrama Classics, Six Plays and How to Stage Them
Sterling Publishing Company, Inc., New York, 1982

Random House Dictionary of the English Language
College Edition
Random House, New York, 1968

Webster's New Twentieth-Century Dictionary of the English Language Unabridged
Second Edition
World Publishing Company, Cleveland and New York, 1971